On the Duties of Merchants

SOURCES IN EARLY MODERN ECONOMICS, ETHICS, AND LAW

Second Series

GENERAL EDITORS

Andrew M. McGinnis
Center for Religion, Culture & Democracy • USA

Wim Decock
UCLouvain and ULiège • Belgium

Continuing in the line of its predecessor, this series publishes original English translations and editions of early modern religious texts in the disciplines of economics, ethics, and law. Representing a variety of confessional traditions and methodological approaches, these texts uncover the foundations of the development of these and related disciplines.

EDITORIAL BOARD

Jordan J. Ballor
Center for Religion, Culture & Democracy • USA

Christiane Birr
Max Planck Institute for Legal History and Legal Theory • Germany

Stephen Bogle
University of Glasgow • Scotland

Alejandro Chafuen
Acton Institute • USA

Ricardo F. Crespo
Universidad Austral and CONICET • Argentina

Virpi Mäkinen
University of Helsinki • Finland

Richard A. Muller
Calvin Theological Seminary • USA

Herman Selderhuis
Theological University Apeldoorn • The Netherlands

John Witte Jr.
Emory University • USA

Zhibin Xie
Tongji University • China

On the Duties of Merchants
Daniel Souterius

Edited by Joost Hengstmengel and Henri Krop
Translated by Albert Gootjes

GRAND RAPIDS · MICHIGAN

On the Duties of Merchants

© 2025 by Joost Hengstmengel and Henri Krop

All rights reserved. No part of this publication may be reproduced, stored in a retrieval system, or transmitted in any form or by any means, including electronic, mechanical, photocopying, recording, or otherwise, without the prior permission of the publisher.

ISBN 978-1-949011-15-9 (hardcover)
ISBN 978-1-949011-16-6 (paperback)
ISBN 978-1-949011-17-3 (ebook)

CLP Academic
   An imprint of the Acton Institute
   for the Study of Religion & Liberty
98 E. Fulton
Grand Rapids, Michigan 49503
616.454.3080
www.acton.org

Interior composition by Judy Schafer
Cover design by Scaturro Design

Contents

Introduction	*vii*
Note on the Translation	*xxix*

On the Duties of Merchants

Dedicatory Epistle		5
Preface		9
The Cause, Matter, and Form of This Work		11
1.	Acquire the Testimony of a Good Conscience	15
2.	Exclude All Pretense and Deceit	23
3.	Pursue the Integrity of Honesty by Avoiding Fraud	31
4.	Pursue the Duties of Justice	43
5.	Pursue Humility of Mind	55
6.	Show Kindness to the Poor	71
7.	Eradicate the Evil of Greed	81
8.	Cut Off the Destructive Thorns of Worry	89
9.	Despise the Love of Earthly Things and Strive for Heavenly Things	105
Conclusion		131
Index		133

Introduction

Joost Hengstmengel
Henri Krop*

De officiis mercatorum (*On the Duties of Merchants, or Learned Discourse on the Most Important Duties of Pious Merchants in Conducting Business*, as per the full English title), offered for the first time in translation here, is not a classic in the common sense of the term. Published in the early seventeenth century, it seems to have ended up primarily in private libraries throughout Europe, judging from early modern catalogues and from the fact that today just over twenty copies survive in public libraries in The Netherlands, Germany, France, and England. It was seldom referred to in contemporary literature[1] and was largely forgotten until Werner Sombart drew attention to its title in his study on the genesis of modern capitalism (and, a little later, by

---

* This introduction builds on our "De gereformeerde religie en economie in de vroege republiek. Daniël Souterius (1571–1634) over de plichten van kooplieden," *Documentatieblad Nadere Reformatie* 42, no. 1 (2018): 2–22; and Joost Hengstmengel, "Het vroege kapitalisme door de ogen van een geleerde dominee: de vier 'economische' werken van Daniel Souterius (1571–1634)," *Documentatieblad Nadere Reformatie* 46, no. 1 (2022): 61–78.

[1] Aside, that is, from the fact that parts of the author's preface were plagiarized in Christophorus Fahrenhorstius, *De bancorottorum pessimo atq; horrendo scelere practico dissertatio politica* (Rostock, 1625).

Introduction

historian Ernst Beins, who failed to get hold of a copy).[2] Nevertheless, this book from the Low Countries is of great historical interest. As one of the earliest, if not the earliest, apologies for commerce in the Dutch Republic, it sheds new light on the early history of Dutch economic thought, whose historiography remains a "black hole" of sorts.[3] In its praise of commerce, it is a predecessor of the famous oration *On the Wise Merchant* from Caspar Barlaeus.

On the Duties of Merchants was published in 1615 at Leiden, a center of humanist learning. Its author, Daniel Souterius, was a Protestant minister. His book can be seen as an attempt to apply a Ciceronian framework of duties to the world of commerce.[4] Cicero's *De officiis* (*On Duties*) enjoyed a newfound popularity in the Renaissance, and proved relevant in a new economic reality.[5] Whereas Cicero had written for his son who studied philosophy, and Ambrose had directed his *De officiis ministrorum* (*On the Duties of Ministers*) to the clergy, Souterius addressed all merchants in Europe. Seeking to offer moral guidance, he discusses the nine duties of merchants: to pursue an up-

---

[2] Werner Sombart, *Der moderne Kapitalismus*, vol. 2, *Das europäische Wirtschaftsleben im Zeitalter des Frühkapitalismus* (Leipzig: Duncker & Humblot, 1917), 24; Ernst Beins, *Die wirtschaftsethik der calvinistischen Kirche der Niederlande 1565–1650* (The Hague: Martinus Nijhoff, 1931), 4n8.

[3] Karel Davids, "Economic Discourse in Europe between Scholasticism and Mandeville: Convergence, Divergence and the Case of the Dutch Republic," in *Departure for Modern Europe: A Handbook of Early Modern Philosophy (1400–1700)*, ed. Hubertus Busche (Hamburg: Felix Meiner, 2011), 81.

[4] On the significance of thinking in terms of duties and offices in the early modern period, see Conal Condren, *Argument and Authority in Early Modern England: The Presupposition of Oaths and Offices* (Cambridge: Cambridge University Press, 2006).

[5] Gloria Vivenza, "The 'Northern' Cicero: On the *Fortuna* of the *De Officiis* in Central Europe," *Mésogeios* 13 (2001): 201–27; idem, "Renaissance Cicero: The 'Economic' Virtues of *De Officiis* I, 22 in Some Sixteenth Century Commentaries," *European Journal of the History of Economic Thought* 11 (2004): 507–23; idem, "Cicero on Economic Subjects," *Journal of the History of Economic Thought* 30 (2008): 385–406.

right conscience, to exclude all pretense and deceit, to avoid cheating and to strive after honesty, to love justice, to put off all pride, to show kindness to the poor, to bridle cupidity, to throw off destructive worries, and to pursue what is of heaven. All these are implied by the basic virtue of *pietas* (sense of duty), which combines an inner-worldly morality with a transcendent perspective. The foreword, which from the perspective of the history of economic thought forms the most interesting part of the work, underlines the usefulness and dignity of commerce. As Souterius stresses, not only common people but also philosophers, princes, and kings practiced trade. The preface is addressed to the directors of the Dutch East India Company (and, in at least one copy, more specifically, to those of the Rotterdam "chamber"), who are presented as an example of honor and honesty in conducting business.

Humanism and Commerce

With no less than 822 references to classical and Christian authorities, *On the Duties of Merchants* is the epitome of humanist learning. Due to a mediocre mind and lack of eloquence, as Souterius expresses it with rhetorical modesty, he thought it best not to use his own words but those of others. More importantly, "whatever is of received authority is of greater weight." Consequently, about half of the main text consists of quotations, most frequently borrowed from Cicero, Lactantius, and Seneca, and not, as promised in the foreword, "from the fertile meadows of the sacred writings." Many of these quotations were in turn taken from by now forgotten anthologies like Joseph Lang's *Loci communes* and Theodor Zwinger's *Theatrum humanae vitae*, which collected memorable sayings from a wide range of Greek and Roman authors that were published by humanist scholars at the time. These collections were of utmost importance to humanist scholarship, since no one had all these rare and precious editions of classical learning directly available to him. While the outside margins of Souterius's book contain references to the sources, the notes in the inside margin summarize the course of the argument. The structure of the argument more generally can also be read and studied from four Ramist tables at the beginning of the book (not included in this edition), as similar tables are also found, for example, in Althusius's *Politica* (1603). They summarize what is discussed in each of the seventy-two chapters, and show how the nine duties of merchants follow, naturally and logically, from observance of the virtue of piety.

The method and style of Souterius's work imitate the better-known *Politica* of Justus Lipsius, which he clearly studied carefully. Published in 1589, the *Politica* is the best example of a *loci communes* (book of common places) that organized and made relevant ancient wisdom for the modern age.[6] Both Souterius and Lipsius apply the so-called *cento* technique. Traditionally a *cento* ("patchwork") was a parodic poem made up of bits from other poems, but Lipsius first applied it to moral-political prose.[7] Echoing Lipsius, Souterius compares his work to a Phrygian tapestry (*aulaeum*). Just like the Phygrians used to weave tapestries out of a variety of colored threads, so he combined ancient sayings and maxims, and merely added "warmth" and "spirit" to them. Souterius also uses the metaphor of a honeycomb. Rather than emulating spiders, who weave their webs from their own entrails, he writes that he composed his book in the manner of bees, who elegantly fill their cells with sweet nectar from the flowers that they visited. Lipsius, in turn, likens his activity to an architect constructing a building from ancient maxims. The two books share virtually the same layout: relatively short chapters abounding with italicized citations, connected by short passages and marginalia from the author.

For an early seventeenth-century text written by a humanist minister, *On the Duties of Merchants* is unexpectedly positive about the merchant's profession. After all, Souterius and his contemporaries were the heirs of a Greek-Roman and Christian tradition that generally

---

[6] "Introduction," in Justus Lipsius, *Politica: Six Books of Politics or Political Instruction*, ed. and trans. Jan Waszink (Assen: Van Gorcum, 2004), 51. See also Ann Moss, "*Monita et Exempla Politica* as Example of a Genre," in *(Un)-masking the Realities of Power: Justus Lipsius and the Dynamics of Political Writing in Early Modern Europe*, ed. Erik De Bom et al. (Leiden: Brill, 2010), 98.

[7] Lipsius, *Politica*, 56–58, 232–33.

regarded trade as a necessary evil or, at best, a mixed blessing.[8] The realm of commerce, and that of retail trade in particular, was associated with vice and deemed unworthy of a self-respecting "free" man. Even though this "fallacy of the ancients" was increasingly criticized in the late Middle Ages and Renaissance, the moral status of the merchant was not a settled question yet. To Souterius, however, there is nothing immoral about commercial activity as such. Quite the contrary, merchants have ample opportunity to put virtue into practice. Thus, commerce does not hinder a pious life, but rather facilitates it. Provided that the duties discussed in this book were taken into account, nothing prevented the merchant from playing a dignified role in the new commercial societies like the Dutch Republic. The products that they market simply are indispensable for the good life.

Interestingly, Souterius's book throughout addresses the "Christian merchant." For one, this implies that he rejected the age-old idea once ascribed to Chrysostom that a merchant can seldom please God and that therefore no Christian should be a merchant.[9] While some of his colleagues still understood the idea of a Christian merchant as an oxymoron (*contradictio in terminis*),[10] Souterius regards commerce as God's gift to humankind. "Nothing," he claims in the foreword, "is more useful, pleasant, and honest for a republic." Moreover, this way of addressing his readers shows that the book is explicitly supraconfessional in nature. There are no traces of a specifically Protestant ethic propagated by some dissenters—as the influential Weber thesis would suggest—or of the thorny issue of predestination. Souterius's duty-based ethics for the merchant is not even exclusively Christian.

---

[8] John W. Baldwin, "The Medieval Theories of Just Price," *Transactions of the American Philosophical Society* 49 (1959): 10–21; Jacob Viner, "Early Attitudes toward Trade and the Merchant," in *Essays on the Intellectual History of Economics*, ed. Douglas A. Irwin (Princeton: Princeton University Press, 1991), 39–44.

[9] Eltjo Schrage, "Mercatura honesta," *Fundamina* 8 (2002): 191–203.

[10] Simon Schama, *The Embarrassment of Riches: An Interpretation of Dutch Culture in the Golden Age* (Berkeley / Los Angeles: University of California Press, 1988), 330.

It is based, so his method suggests, on the *consensus gentium* and hence the divine order of things. But since for Souterius truth is one, there can be no contradiction between Christian and pagan wisdom.

Life and Times of Daniel Souterius

Daniel Souterius (also written as De Zouter, Souter, Zouterius, Sauter, Sauterius) was born in Dover, England, on 27 August 1571, where his Flemish parents may have gone to escape religious persecution.[11] A contemporary source from the same year mentions the presence "in a howse of John Knappe's" of "Jessper de Souter, his wif and ij chelderne, merchauntes."[12] After his return to Flanders, Daniel's father, Jaspar de Souter (1525–1579), came to hold various government offices in Dunkirk and Ostend. He eventually sent his son to the Latin school in Flushing.

In 1572, many years before Daniel Souterius arrived there, Flushing became the second town of the Netherlands to side with the Reformation. The year 1572 also was the beginning of the armed Dutch Revolt against its legitimate prince Philip II, the king of Spain. Daniel's father would later play a role in this revolt in his function of bailiff of Ostend. In 1579 seven provinces that set themselves in rebellion to the Habsburg Empire signed a defense treaty called the Union of Utrecht. This year marks the creation of the Republic of the Seven United Netherlands, which lasted to the Napoleonic Age. In terms of religion, the Union of Utrecht determined that the provinces had

---

[11] "Souter of Souterius (Daniel)," in *Biographisch Woordenboek der Nederlanden*, vol. 17-2, ed. A. J. van der Aa (Haarlem: J. van Brederode, 1874), 868–70. While Souterius matriculated at Leiden University as "Londinensis," one of the disputations he defended lists "Davernas," Latin for Dover, as his place of birth. The latter fact is confirmed in Daniël Souterius, *Palamedes; sive de tabula lusoria, alea, et variis ludis* (Leiden, 1622), "Epistola dedicatoria": "Sum natione Anglus, ex Flandricis parentibus oriundus: natus in Oppido Doverensi, quod est in tractu Cantii, portus opportunitate celebratissimum."

[12] G. H. Overend, "Strangers at Dover," *Proceedings of the Huguenot Society of London* (13 November 1889 and 8 January 1890): 161.

to choose a public religion, "provided that each person shall remain free in his religion and that no one shall be investigated or persecuted because of his religion." In due time all seven provinces chose the Reformed Church as their religion, although it was not until the end of the seventeenth century that the Reformed Church represented a clear majority among the inhabitants of the Dutch provinces.

At the age of twenty-one, Souterius matriculated at the new university at Leiden, established in 1575 as reward for the hardships the city had endured during a long siege by Spanish troops. The pamphlets of the academic disputations that he defended at Leiden show the continuing link with Flushing. In 1594 he defended a disputation on faith, which is dedicated to two ministers in Zeeland, Johannes Belosius and Aegidius Bursius, for some time vice-principal of the Flushing Latin school. Two years later he defended a disputation under the presidency of the theologian Gomarus, who later resigned from his office in the wake of the Arminian controversy. This pamphlet is dedicated to the four ministers of the Flushing church.[13]

As noted, the recently established university of Leiden was a center of Renaissance humanism. The founding fathers spared no trouble or expense to attract world-famous humanists such as Joseph Justus Scaliger, who only agreed to come on the condition that he would not have to teach, and Lipsius. Souterius's Leiden education made him a humanist. He corresponded on scholarly matters with that luminary of humanist learning, Gerard Vossius.[14] Humanism not only provided the old *trivium* with a new and more ambitious name (*studia humanitatis,* which gave the movement its name), but also increased its actual scope, content, and significance in the curriculum of the schools and universities. It transformed the study of texts, both sacred and classic,

---

[13] Daniel Zouterius, *Theses theologicae de fide* (Leiden, 1594), A1v; idem, *Disputationum theologicarum tertia, de Sacrae Scripturae perspicuitate* (Leiden, 1596), Av.

[14] The Special Collections of the Amsterdam University Library (HSS-mag.: III E 5: 149) hold a letter from Vossius to Souterius dated 27 November 1621, which contains corrections of Greek quotations and suggestions for better translations into Latin.

into a scholarly discipline and stimulated the study of Greek, Hebrew, and history. The combination of Protestantism—one of the main objectives of the university was the training of Reformed ministers for the new Republic—and a humanist zeal, which we find in Souterius as well, should come as no surprise. According to the *History of the Reformed Churches in the French Kingdom* of Calvin's fellow reformer Theodore Beza, the Reformation started not with Luther but with the German humanist John Reuchlin, who had made knowledge of Hebrew available to the Church. Thus, Christians regained the ability to read the divine truths, now in their original form and languages.

Souterius started his ecclesiastical career as a pastoral candidate at Hillegom and afterwards served the congregations of Kampen and Haarlem, where he died in 1634. In 1615 he left Kampen due to the theological conflict between Gomarists and Arminians. In the Dutch Republic the controversy started with Jacobus Arminius, who as minister at Amsterdam in the 1590s began to criticize Beza's view on predestination. Arminius attempted to reconcile divine predestination with (limited) human free will. After his death the States of Holland asked his supporters to summarize their views in the five articles of the Remonstrance, which gave them their name "Remonstrants." While the States of Holland invited their ministers to sign it, other provinces of the Dutch Republic rejected the Remonstrance. The latter theological-political party was therefore called the "Counter-Remonstrants." Maurice, the Prince of Orange and commander of the army of the Republic, sided with them. In 1618 the "National" Synod of Dordrecht convened and condemned the Remonstrance. Arminian ministers had to recant their views, or else go into exile.

Kampen was an Arminian city. Souterius, however, sided with the Gomarists and in 1615 caused a stir with a sermon on the doctrine of predestination.[15] Once the church service had finished, advo-

---

[15] J. Veenhof, "Het remonstrantisme te Kampen tot de regeringsverandering in 1620," *Kamper Almanak* (1957–58): 261–62; Christiaan Ravensbergen, "Commotie in Kampen. De rechtzinnigheid en naaktloperij van Georgius Goyckerus, predikant te Wilsum (1611–1623)," *Kamper Almanak* (2006): 110–13.

cates and opponents met each other below the pulpit. They began to shout and fight, and a sword was even drawn, as an eyewitness described the events in his *Kerklicke gheschiedenissen* (*Ecclesiastical Histories*).[16] The next day the fight continued at the town-hall. One month later Souterius left Kampen for Haarlem. Although Haarlem had no Arminian ministers, Souterius reentered the conflict there. The city magistracy wanted to introduce a new church order that would acknowledge the authority of the civil magistracy in the government of the church, the so-called *ius circa sacra*. Souterius opposed this measure and denounced this attempt to introduce "novelties" into the Church. The result was a schism in the Haarlem congregation.[17]

Souterius as a Writer on Economics

Souterius was a prolific writer. A contemporary wrote verses in which he claimed that Souterius "endlessly makes books and fills the terrestrial globe / with many brave writings, by which he will live on after his death," before going on to list a dozen book titles, half in the vernacular and half in Latin.[18] Nineteen works, including collections of sermons, poems, and six *cento* works, have survived. Some modern scholars associate Souterius with the "Further Reformation," which was propagated in the Netherlands by the influential Utrecht theologian Voetius. They believe that Souterius wanted to force upon society an oppressive program of strictness (*precisitas*), pointing to his book against drunkenness and another on games. Indeed, according to Souterius the Reformation did not imply a reform of doctrine only, but should result in a reform of society as well. However, for him such

---

[16] Wilhelmus Baudartius, *Memoryen ofte Cort Verhael Der Gedenckweerdichste so kercklicke als werltlicke gheschiedenissen* (Zutphen, 1624), VII, 5–6.

[17] J. Spaans, *Haarlem na de reformatie. Stedelijke cultuur en kerkelijk leven 1577–1620* (Leiden: Stichting Hollandse historische reeks, 1989), 216.

[18] Samuel Ampzing, *Beschryvinge ende lof der stad Haerlem in Holland* (Haarlem, 1628), 133–35.

reform is not a duty that belongs to the magistrate. The norms of a Christian life can only be determined by one's own conscience.

In addition to poems in praise of the House of Orange, sermons, and a few moralistic treatises, Souterius produced no less than three works discussing economic subjects. The first, *De officiis mercatorum*, he finished "in Kampen, 18 March 1615, in my study." In the same year, two days later to be precise, he sent to press his *Praxis banccaeruptorum huius seculi* (*Practice of the Bankrupters of Our Age*). This book was the most influential of the three: it appeared in a second edition and was translated into German and English.[19] Often these two works are found bound together as a single volume. In 1622 Souterius published *Paedagogus divitum, de luxu, et vero opum usu* (*The Educator of the Rich: On Luxury and the True Use of Property*). All of these three books have the same layout and are based on the same *cento* technique discussed above. In *Praxis*, dedicated to the councilors of the Court of Holland, Souterius deals with the evil practices of those who default on their debts and with the damage they bring about for fellow people and society. He carefully distinguishes between traders who lose their capital due to unforeseen circumstances and merchants who by their own fault, and even by premeditation, are in default. His work focuses on the latter group. According to Souterius, these traders are unworthy of the honourable name *mercator*. Such unreliable and fraudulent people are truly called *banccaeruptores*, as he unusually explains, because they break (*rumpere*) the duty of appearing at the tables or benches (*bancae*) of their creditors. Bankrupters are only interested in their own profit, and squeeze money from their fellow men, spend it like water, and do not fulfil their promise to refund the capital borrowed. Such practices undermine the very foundations of society. They prefer their private interest above public welfare and render serious damage to commerce, which according to Aristotle and Cicero is of vital importance to the preservation of mankind.

---

[19] Daniel Sauter, *Practica der Bancarottierer, Das ist Eigentliche, lebhaffte Entwerffung der wunderlichen Practicen, der Bancarottierer und Falliten, zu disen unsern zeiten* (Ausburg, 1615); idem, *The Practise of the Banckrupts of these Times* (London, 1640).

Although the *Paedagogus* was written in Kampen, it was published during Souterius's Haarlem ministry. In the dedication to Job Paludanus, the court physician of the czar, he maintains that we should approve of wealth because "all goods originate in divine benevolence." When we abuse property, however, it is the source of many evils and "by an abundance of wealth the vigorous and virtuous parts of soul will be easily dragged along by the maelstrom of vice." This danger is eminent in the United Provinces, Souterius observes, where the excessive growth of wealth stimulates love of luxury. Only the typically Dutch virtue of modesty will be able to keep our use of wealth within the boundaries established by human and divine laws. Souterius then goes on to discuss the proper measure of clothing, architecture, furniture, food, and drink, as well as gambling games. Strikingly, Souterius does not urge the necessity of ascesis at all, but merely pleads for compliance with the golden mean.

The fact that Souterius published the book during his Haarlem period was a prudent choice. According to the Arminian writer of the *Kerkelicke historie* (*Ecclesiastical History*), Souterius became embroiled in controversy at Kampen not so much due to his Counter-Remonstrant leanings as his "worldly" lifestyle. Both he and his wife, a cloth merchant's daughter, had "a magnificent housekeeping and expensive clothes, which gave great offence. That is why he was often derided and reproved."[20] Apparently the Kampen minister easily combined a luxurious lifestyle and open mind to commerce with doctrinal strictness.

Place in the History of Economic Thought

It is not that easy to place *On the Duties of Merchants* in one of the "economic" genres of the early modern period. Clearly the book cannot be classified as a contribution to the science of political economy as it emerged at that time. In spite of what the title might suggest, Souterius does not engage with practical or theoretical issues in trade. If such matters as money, wealth, and fair trade come up at all, they are

---

[20] Johannes Uytenbogaert, *De Kerckelicke historie, Vervatende verscheyden gedenckwaerdige saecken, Inde Christenheyt voorgevallen* (s.l., 1646), 635.

INTRODUCTION

only mentioned in passing. References to contemporary mercantilists or neo-scholastic writers on economics are altogether absent from the work. The closest are a few quotations from the *Tractatus de mercatura seu mercatore* (*Treatise on Commerce or the Merchant*, 1553) of Benvenuto Straccha or Stracca, the Italian "father of commercial law."[21] However, it is not to the practical parts dealing with mercantile contracts, maritime law, and bankruptcy that Souterius refers, but rather the second part where Straccha discusses the nobility of the merchant and his rights and duties, as imposed by religion and canon law. The latter, of course, were the subjects that the Dutch minister was most interested in himself, and it is clear that he had one of the editions of Straccha's work in front of him when he compiled his own.

On closer observation, Souterius's *Duties* shows resemblances with at least three—partly overlapping!—genres. The first is that of practical mercantile handbooks.[22] Books like these were meant as professional manuals for merchants and dealt with foreign currencies, weights and exchange rates, geography, bookkeeping, etc. In the late medieval and early modern period, hundreds of such *ars mercatoria* works appeared in Europe.[23] Souterius's book is reminiscent of a small number of them

---

[21] Andrea Romano, "Stracca, Benvenuto (1509–1578)," in *The Oxford International Encyclopedia of Legal History*, ed. Stanley N. Katz (Oxford: Oxford University Press, 2009), https://doi.org/10.1093/acref/9780195134056.001.0001; Stefania Gialdroni, "Stracca, Treatise on Commerce," in *The Formation and Transmission of Western Legal Culture: 150 Books That Made the Law in the Age of Printing*, ed. Serge Dauchy et al. (Cham: Springer, 2016), 96–99.

[22] Eugen Leitherer, *Geschichte der Handels- und Absatzwirtschaftlichen Literatur* (Köln: Westdeutscher Verlag, 1961), chs. 3–4. See also *Kaufmannsbücher und Handelspraktiken vom Spätmittelalter bis zum 20. Jahrhundert*, ed. Markus A. Denzel et al. (Stuttgart: Steiner, 2002); *Understanding the Sources of Early Modern and Modern Commercial Law*, ed. Heikki Pihlajamäki et al. (Leiden: Brill Nijhoff, 2018).

[23] *Ars Mercatoria. Handbücher und Traktate für den Gebrauch des Kaufmanns. Eine analytische Bibliographie*, ed. Jochen Hoock and Pierre Jeannin (Paderborn: Schöningh, 1991–93).

that offered reflections on the duties of merchants in addition to practical advice.[24] Straccha's *Treatise* is one of them, but the closest example may actually be *Della mercatura et del mercante perfetto* (*On Commerce and the Perfect Merchant*) from the Ragusan merchant and humanist Benedetto Cotrugli. Written around 1458 and published more than a century later, it can be seen as the first "mirror of merchants."[25] It has a part on the merchant's religious duties, and one on his moral duties, or "the moral and civil conduct of life according to the virtues attendant on human civilization, a quality essential to any good merchant."[26] Like Souterius, Cotrugli discusses the virtues of justice, temperance, and liberality, with constant reference to ancient writers, medieval theologians, and Holy Scripture.

The second genre is that of Christian business ethics. A seventeenth-century book catalogue lists Souterius's book among several other *mercatura* works, mostly in the German language, that have the *mercator Christianus* as their subject.[27] What they offered was a specifically spiritual mirror for merchants. Unfortunately, one of the manuals that predates Souterius—*Geistliche und weltliche Kauffmannschafft* (*Spiritual and Worldly Commerce*, 1605)—seems to be lost. The same is true for a text with the promising title *Moraale beroerende de amptsplicht des christelyken coopmans* (*Moral touching the Christian Merchant's*

---

[24] Cf. Jochen Hoock, "Professional Ethics and Commercial Rationality at the Beginning of the Modern Era," in *The Self-Perception of Early Modern Capitalists*, ed. Margareth C. Jacob and Catharine Secretan (New York: Palgrave Macmillan, 2008), 147–59.

[25] Catherine Secretan, "From 'Permutation of Commodities' to the Praise of 'Doux Commerce': Changes in Economic Rationality in Early Modern Times," in *History of Economic Rationalities: Economic Reasoning as Knowledge and Practice Authority*, ed. Jakob Bek-Thomsen et al. (Cham: Springer, 2017), 15.

[26] Benedetto Cotrugli, *The Book of the Art of Trade*, ed. Carlo Carraro and Giovanni Favero (Cham: Springer, 2017), 111.

[27] Martin Lipenius, *Bibliotheca realis universalis* (Frankfurt, 1685), 273–74.

Duty, 1583) mentioned elsewhere.[28] An early example of a Christian business ethics that has survived is Coornhert's *De Coopman* (*The Merchant*, 1580), a humanistic dialogue on conducting business in a Christian, godly manner.[29] According to Coornhert, himself the son of an Amsterdam clothier, commerce is neither good nor evil, since it belongs to the indifferent matters, as the Stoics call it. This implies that Christians may engage in it, as long as they obey the will of God and their own conscience. Thereafter, Coornhert discusses the Christian merchant's main virtues as well as some vices that must be avoided at all costs. A good and honest merchant, Coornhert argues, is no less than an "image of Christ."

A subclass of the second genre was formed by pietistic seaman's vade-mecums.[30] These handbooks, literally to be taken on board merchant ships, offered advice on how to act as Christian seafarers. They mostly came in the form of collections of sermons. This typically Dutch genre had a precursor in *Seefarer Trost* (*Seafarer Consolation*, 1579) from the German Lutheran Stephan Praetorius.[31] In the seventeenth-century Dutch Republic, ministers of the Further Reformation produced six of these vademecums, the first of which was published in 1611. Like *On the Duties of Merchants*, some of them were dedicated

---

[28] It is mentioned in *De koopman, of, bydragen ten opbouw van Neêrlands koophandel en zeevaard* 1, no. 54 (1768): 426, where it is ascribed to Hendrik Laurenszoon Spiegel.

[29] [Dirck Volkertsz. Coornhert], *De Coopman. Aenwysende doprechte conste, om Christelyck ende met eenen ghelycken moede int winnen en verliesen, Coophandel te drijven* (Haarlem, 1580), 44–45.

[30] L. F. Groenendijk, "Pietistische vademecums voor zeevarenden," *Documentatieblad Nadere Reformatie* 11/4 (1987): 126–39; A. Th. Boone, "'Om een woesten hoop te brengen tot de kerck'. Een onderzoek naar zend-ingsgedachten in piëtistische zeemansvademecums," in *Zending tussen woord en daad. Twee hoofdstukken uit de geschiedenis van gereformeerd piëtisme en zending* (Kampen: De Groot Goudriaan, 1991), 12–46.

[31] Cf. Stephan Praetorius, *Fluctus et Luctus Marini, Das ist: Nützlicher Unterricht. wie sich all Christlich Seefahrende Kaufleut, und Gottselige Schiffer … fromm und bescheidenlich … seyn sollen* (Frankfurt, 1608).

to the directors of the East or West India Company. The best example and "flagship" of the genre, which is also most similar to Souterius's treatise, is *'t Geestelyck roer van't coopmans schip* (*The Spiritual Rudder of the Merchant Ship*, 1638). This treatise by the Zealand minister Godefridus Udemans discusses a variety of subjects, including the origin and utility of commerce and the reasonableness of slavery. One part is devoted to the "office of merchants," dealing with the question how a merchant should behave in a godly manner. It may be no coinci-dence that both he and Souterius take their starting point in Titus 2:11–12 ("For the grace of God that brings salvation has appeared to all men, teaching us that, denying ungodliness and worldly lusts, we should live soberly, righteously, and godly in the present age"). Unlike his colleague, however, Udemans primarily bases his reflections on such virtues as honesty, justice, and temperance on Scripture.

The third genre with which the book, and especially its foreword, can be associated is that of the humanist apologies for commerce, books that justified and commended commerce on theological-philosophical grounds. To our knowledge, one of the earliest examples is the *Pragmatologia* (1606) by the German minister Johannes Sommerus. The subtitle of the book perfectly summarizes his mission: "thorough and detailed account of the laudable commerce [*Kauffmanschafft*], of its origin, development, necessity, and many uses: from God's Word, imperial and papal rights, treatises of famous jurists, books of highly learned philosophers and poets." Sommerus's justification of commerce draws not only on Bible texts and classical authorities but also on modern writers like Bodin and Lipsius. Yet the best-known text in this genre is *Mercator sapiens* (*The Wise Merchant*, 1633).[32] In this Latin oration, held at the opening of the Illustrious School of Amsterdam, the humanist minister Caspar Barlaeus argued for the close connection between commerce and the study of philosophy. Historically speaking

---

[32] For a new critical edition, see Caspar Barlaeus, *The Wise Merchant*, ed. Anna-Luna Post, trans. Corinna Vermeulen (Amsterdam: Amsterdam University Press, 2019). Also helpful is the extensive introduction in Catherine Secretan, *Le «marchand philosophe» de Caspar Barlaeus. Un éloge du commerce dans la Hollande du Siècle d'Or* (Paris: Honoré Champion, 2002).

philosophy benefitted from the growth of commerce, and vice versa philosophy proves of great use to the merchant. The ideal merchant indeed is a wise merchant. The "virtues and duties of merchants" that Barlaeus discusses all revolve around wisdom. They need wisdom to distinguish between honest and dishonest profits, to cure them from vices like greed and intemperance, and to grasp the Ciceronian idea that the expedient and the morally right are two sides of the same coin.

Perhaps it is safest to say that Souterius's treatise is a mirror for Christian merchants, a business ethics, and a humanist apology for commerce all in one. That said, it is very much the question whether it reached the target audience of the first two genres, namely practicing merchants. After all, *On the Duties of Merchants* was written in scholarly Latin. Even though this *lingua franca* was the best choice to address merchants all over Europe, as was Souterius's stated intention, it was actually a language that few merchants understood.[33] Their lack of higher education precisely made Cotrugli compose his work on the perfect merchant in the vernacular rather than in elegant Latin.[34] It might therefore be that Souterius had a similar hidden agenda as Barlaeus, who likewise addressed an audience of partly "respected citizens and merchants" in humanistic Latin. Their works can be seen as attempts to come to terms with the commercial expansion of the Dutch Republic.[35] Both of them sought to legitimize the mercantile pursuit of wealth, against the background of the ancient mistrust of commercial activity. By dedicating his work to the directors of the East India Company and praising the moral standards of their merchants, Souterius more specifically defended the right of the provinces

---

[33] Willem Frijhoff, "La formation des négociants de la République hollandaise," in *Cultures et formations négociantes dans l'Europe moderne*, ed. Franco Angiolini and Daniel Roche (Paris: EHESS, 1995), 175–98.

[34] See the preface in Cotrugli, *The Book of the Art of Trade*, 26.

[35] Harold J. Cook, *Matters of Exchange: Commerce, Medicine, and Science in the Dutch Golden Age* (New Haven / London: Yale University Press, 2007), 68–73; Arthur Weststeijn, *Commercial Republicanism in the Dutch Golden Age: The Political Thought of Johan & Pieter de la Court* (Leiden / Boston: Brill, 2012), 184–90.

of Holland and Zeeland to continue their long-distance trade. This endeavor made him an ally of that other famous Dutchman, Hugo Grotius.

Bibliography

Primary Sources

Ampzing, Samuel. *Beschryvinge ende lof der stad Haerlem in Holland*. Haarlem, 1628.

Barlaeus, Caspar. *The Wise Merchant*. Edited by Anna-Luna Post. Translated by Corinna Vermeulen. Amsterdam: Amsterdam University Press, 2019.

Baudartius, Wilhelmus. *Memoryen ofte Cort Verhael Der Gedenck-weerdichste so kercklicke als werltlicke gheschiedenissen*. Zutphen, 1624.

Coornhert, Dirck Volkertszoon. *De Coopman. Aenwysende doprechte conste, om Christelyck ende met eenen ghelycken moede int winnen en verliesen, Coophandel te drijven*. Haarlem, 1580.

Cotrugli, Benedetto. *The Book of the Art of Trade*. Edited by Carlo Carraro and Giovanni Favero. Cham: Springer, 2017.

Fahrenhorstius, Christophorus. *De bancorottorum pessimo atq; horrendo scelere practico dissertatio politica*. Rostock, 1625.

De koopman, of, bydragen ten opbouw van Neêrlands koophandel en zeevaard, vol. 1. Amsterdam, 1768.

Lipenius, Martin. *Bibliotheca realis universalis*. Frankfurt, 1685.

Lipsius, Justus. *Politica: Six Books of Politics or Political Instruction*. Edited and translated by Jan Waszink. Assen: Van Gorcum, 2004.

Praetorius, Stephan. *Fluctus et Luctus Marini, Das ist: Nützlicher Unterricht. wie sich all Christlich Seefahrende Kaufleut, und Gottselige Schiffer … fromm und bescheidenlich … seyn sollen*. Frankfurt, 1608.

Sauter, Daniel. *Practica der Bancarottierer, Das ist Eigentliche, lebhaffte Entwerffung der wunderlichen Practicen, der Bancarottierer und Falliten, zu disen unsern zeiten*. Ausburg, 1615.

———. *The Practise of the Banckrupts of these Times*. London, 1640.

Introduction

Souterius, Daniël. *Palamedes; sive de tabula lusoria, alea, et variis ludis.* Leiden, 1622.

Uytenbogaert, Johannes. *De Kerckelicke historie, Vervatende verscheyden gedenckwaerdige saecken, Christenheyt voorgevallen.* s.l., 1646.

Zouterius, Daniel. *Theses theologicae de fide.* Leiden, 1594.

———. *Disputationum theologicarum tertia, de Sacrae Scripturae perspicuitate.* Leiden, 1596.

Secondary Sources

Baldwin, John W. "The Medieval Theories of Just Price." *Transactions of the American Philosophical Society* 49 (1959): 10–21.

Beins, Ernst. *Die wirtschaftsethik der calvinistischen Kirche der Niederlande 1565–1650.* The Hague: Martinus Nijhoff, 1931.

Boone, A. Th. "'Om een woesten hoop te brengen tot de kerck'. Een onderzoek naar zendingsgedachten in piëtistische zeemansvademecums." In *Zending tussen woord en daad. Twee hoofdstukken uit de geschiedenis van gereformeerd piëtisme en zending,* 12–46. Kampen: De Groot Goudriaan, 1991.

Condren, Conal. *Argument and Authority in Early Modern England: The Presupposition of Oaths and Offices.* Cambridge: Cambridge University Press, 2006.

Cook, Harold J. *Matters of Exchange: Commerce, Medicine, and Science in the Dutch Golden Age.* New Haven / London: Yale University Press, 2007.

Davids, Karel. "Economic Discourse in Europe between Scholasticism and Mandeville: Convergence, Divergence and the Case of the Dutch Republic." In *Departure for Modern Europe: A Handbook of Early Modern Philosophy (1400–1700),* edited by Hubertus Busche, 80–95. Hamburg: Felix Meiner, 2011.

Denzel, Markus A., Jean Claude Hocquet and Harald Witthöft, eds. *Kaufmanns-bücher und Handelspraktiken vom Spätmittelalter bis zum 20. Jahrhundert.* Stuttgart: Steiner, 2002.

Frijhoff, Willem. "La formation des négociants de la République hollandaise." In *Cultures et formations négociantes dans l'Europe moderne,* edited by Franco Angiolini and Daniel Roche, 175–98. Paris: EHESS, 1995.

Gialdroni, Stefania. "Stracca, Treatise on Commerce." In *The Formation and Transmission of Western Legal Culture: 150 Books That Made the Law in the Age of Printing*, edited by Serge Dauchy, Georges Martyn, Anthony Musson, Heikki Pihlajamäki, and Alain Wijffels, 96–99. Cham: Springer, 2016.

Groenendijk, L. F. "Pietistische vademecums voor zeevarenden." *Documentatieblad Nadere Reformatie* 11, no. 4 (1987): 126–39.

Hengstmengel, Joost. "Bankruptcy in the Golden Age of Dutch Calvinism: The Pioneering Works of Daniel Sauterius (1571–1634)." In *Debt or Sin? The Moral Roots of European Legal and Economic Thought*, edited by Wim Decock. Leiden: Brill, forthcoming.

———. "Het vroege kapitalisme door de ogen van een geleerde dominee: de vier 'economische werken' van Daniël Souterius (1571–1634)." *Documentatieblad Nadere Reformatie* 46, no. 1 (2022): 61–78.

Hengstmengel, Joost, and Henri Krop. "De gereformeerde religie en economie in de vroege republiek. Daniël Souterius (1571–1634) over de plichten van kooplieden." *Documentatieblad Nadere Reformatie* 42, no. 1 (2018): 2–22.

Hoock, Jochen. "Professional Ethics and Commercial Rationality at the Beginning of the Modern Era." In *The Self-Perception of Early Modern Capitalists*, edited by Margareth C. Jacob and Catharine Secretan, 147–59. New York: Palgrave Macmillan, 2008.

Hoock, Jochen, and Pierre Jeannin, eds. *Ars Mercatoria. Handbücher und Traktate für den Gebrauch des Kaufmanns. Eine analytische Bibliographie.* Paderborn: Schöningh, 1991–1993.

Leitherer, Eugen. *Geschichte der Handels- und Absatzwirtschaftlichen Literatur.* Köln: Westdeutscher Verlag, 1961.

Moss, Ann. "*Monita et Exempla Politica* as Example of a Genre." In *(Un)masking the Realities of Power: Justus Lipsius and the Dynamics of Political Writing in Early Modern Europe*, edited by Erik De Bom, Marijke Janssens, Toon Van Houdt, and Jan Papy, 95–114. Leiden: Brill, 2010.

Overend, G. H. "Strangers at Dover." *Proceedings of the Huguenot Society of London* (13 November 1889 and 8 January 1890): 91–171.

Introduction

Pihlajamäki, Heikki, Albrecht Cordes, Serge Dauchy, and Dave De ruysscher, eds. *Understanding the Sources of Early Modern and Modern Commercial Law*. Leiden: Brill Nijhoff, 2018.

Ravensbergen, Christiaan. "Commotie in Kampen. De rechtzinnigheid en naaktloperij van Georgius Goyckerus, predikant te Wilsum (1611–1623)." *Kamper Almanak* (2006): 110–13.

Romano, Andrea. "Stracca, Benvenuto (1509–1578)." In *The Oxford International Encyclopedia of Legal History*, edited by Stanley N. Katz. Oxford: Oxford University Press, 2009. https://doi.org/10.1093/acref/9780195134056.001.0001.

Schrage, Eltjo. "Mercatura honesta." *Fundamina* 8 (2002): 191–203.

Schama, Simon. *The Embarrassment of Riches: An Interpretation of Dutch Culture in the Golden Age*. Berkeley / Los Angeles: University of California Press, 1988.

Secretan, Catherine. "From 'Permutation of Commodities' to the Praise of 'Doux Commerce': Changes in Economic Rationality in Early Modern Times." In *History of Economic Rationalities: Economic Reasoning as Knowledge and Practice Authority*, edited by Jakob Bek-Thomsen et al., 13–20. Cham: Springer, 2017.

———. *Le «marchand philosophe» de Caspar Barlaeus. Un éloge du commerce dans la Hollande du Siècle d'Or*. Paris: Honoré Champion, 2002.

Sombart, Werner. *Der moderne Kapitalismus*, vol. 2, *Das europäische Wirtschaftsleben im Zeitalter des Frühkapitalismus*. Leipzig: Duncker & Humblot, 1917.

Spaans, J. *Haarlem na de reformatie. Stedelijke cultuur en kerkelijk leven 1577–1620*. Leiden: Stichting Hollandse historische reeks, 1989.

Van der Aa, A. J., ed. *Biographisch Woordenboek der Nederlanden*, vol. 17. Haarlem: J. van Brederode, 1874.

Veenhof, J. "Het remonstrantisme te Kampen tot de regeringsverandering in 1620." *Kamper Almanak* (1957–58): 261–62.

Viner, Jacob. "Early Attitudes toward Trade and the Merchant." In *Essays on the Intellectual History of Economics*, edited by Douglas A. Irwin, 39–44. Princeton: Princeton University Press, 1991.

Vivenza, Gloria. "Cicero on Economic Subjects." *Journal of the History of Economic Thought* 30 (2008): 385–406.

———. "The 'Northern' Cicero: On the *Fortuna* of the *De Officiis* in Central Europe." *Mésogeios* 13 (2001): 201–27.

———. "Renaissance Cicero: The 'Economic' Virtues' of *De Officiis* I, 22 in Some Sixteenth Century Commentaries." *European Journal of the History of Economic Thought* 11 (2004): 507–23.

Weststeijn, Arthur. *Commercial Republicanism in the Dutch Golden Age: The Political Thought of Johan & Pieter de la Court*. Leiden: Brill, 2012.

Note on the Translation

This book presents a full translation of Daniel Sauterius, *De Officijs mercatorvm, Sive diatribae, quae praecipua Mercatorum Pietatis inter Negociandum continent officia* (Leiden: Johannes van Dorp, printed by Johannes Maire, 1615). The four analytical tables, the notes in the inside margin summarizing the argument, and the extensive table of contents (index) were not included. All of Souterius's references in the outside margin have been converted to footnotes and expanded as complete, modern references.

The original work contains seventy-two chapters, most of which are very short by modern standards. These chapter divisions, along with their original numbering, have been retained in this translation, but they have been set as sections instead of chapters. A broader structure of nine chapters has been imposed. This follows the high-level outline that Souterius himself presents in his one-page preface. This chapter structure helps the modern reader more easily grasp the flow of Souterius's argument from the table of contents, and it makes the layout of the book more conventional and useful.

All information in square brackets […], both in the main text and footnotes, has been added by the translator or editors.

For quotations from ancient and medieval sources, modern translations were consulted where available, as credited in the footnotes. These have, however, been revised tacitly as needed to match the style and vocabulary of the present translation. For Bible texts, the New King James Version was used, though these quotations also have been revised tacitly in some instances. All other translations are the translator's. The footnote references to existing translations also serve as findings aids; where no such translation was available, references keyed to standard critical texts have been supplied. The following abbreviations, followed in the notes by volume and page number, have been used for some of the most frequently cited English translations:

ACW — *Ancient Christian Writers* (New York / Mahwah: Paulist Press, 1946–)

CF — *Cistercian Fathers series* (Spencer: Cistercian Publications, 1970–)

CWE — *Collected Works of Erasmus*, vols. 31–36, *Adages* (Toronto / Buffalo / London: University of Toronto Press, 1982–2016)

FC — *The Fathers of the Church: A New Translation* (Washington: Catholic University of America Press, 1947–)

LCL — *Loeb Classical Library* (London: William Heinemann / Cambridge: Harvard University Press, 1912–)

MPG — *Patrologia Graeca* (Paris: Migne, 1856–1857)

MPL — *Patrologia Latina* (Paris: Migne, 1844–1855)

NPNF1/2 — (Buffalo: Christian Literature Company / New York: Charles Scribner, 1886–1900)

WSA — *The Works of Saint Augustine: A Translation for the 21st Century* (Hyde Park, NY: New City Press, 1990–)

NOTE ON THE TRANSLATION

In addition, the following translations were consulted:

Barnish	Cassiodorus, *Variae*, trans. S.J.B. Barnish, Translated Texts for Historians (Liverpool: Liverpool University Press, 1992)
Blakeney	Lactantius, *Firmiani Lactantii Epitome institutionum divinarum: Lactantius' Epitome of the Divine Institutes*, trans. Edward H. Blakeney (London: SPCK, 1950)
Blume	*The Codex of Justinian: A New Annotated Translation, with Parallel Latin and Greek Text*, ed. Bruce W. Frier, based on trans. Fred H. Blume, 3 vols. (Cambridge: Cambridge University Press, 2016)
Davidson	Ambrose, *De Officiis: Edited with an Introduction, Translation, and Commentary*, ed. and trans. Ivor J. Davidson, Oxford Early Christian Studies, 2 vols. (Oxford: Oxford University Press, 2002)
Evans	Bernard of Clairvaux, *Selected Works*, trans. Gillian R. Evans, The Classics of Western Spirituality (New York: Paulist Press, 1987)—for *Liber de gradibus humilitatis et superbiae*
James	*The Letters of Saint Bernard of Clairvaux*, trans. Bruno Scott James (London: Burns Oates, 1953)
Kerns	Gregory the Great, *Moral Reflections on the Book of Job*, trans. Brian Kerns, Cistercian Studies, 6 vols. (Collegeville: Liturgical Press, 2014–)
Leclercq	Bernard of Clairvaux, *S. Bernardi Opera*, ed. Jean Leclercq and Henri M. Rochais, 7 vols. (Rome: Editiones Cistercienses, 1957–1972)

Note on the Translation

Newton — Cicero, *On Duties*, trans. Benjamin Patrick Newton, Agora Editions (Ithaca / London: Cornell University Press, 2016).

Sanford — Salvian, *On the Government of God: A Treatise Wherein are Shown by Argument and by Examples Drawn from the Abandoned Society of the Times the Ways of God Toward his Creatures*, trans. Eva M. Sanford (New York: Columbia University Press, 1930).

Silano — Peter Lombard, *The Sentences*, trans. Giulio Silano, Medieval Sources in Translation (Toronto: Pontifical Institute of Medieval Studies, 2008).

Stahl — Macrobius, *Commentary on the Dream of Scipio*, ed. and trans. William H. Stahl, Records of Civilization: Sources and Studies (New York: Columbia University Press, 1952).

Waszink — Lipsius, *Politica: Six Books of Politics or Political Instruction*, ed. and trans. Jan. Waszink (Assen: Van Gorcum, 2004).

On the Duties of Merchants

De Officijs
MERCATORVM,
Sive
DIATRIBAE,
quæ præcipua Mercatorum Pietatis inter Negociandum
continent officia;

Auctore DANIELE SAVTERIO.

LVGDVNI BATAVORVM,
Ex Officina Ioannis à Dorp, 1615.
Proſtant apud Iohannem Maire.

(Image courtesy of Utrecht University Library, ODG 4754 dl 2)

Dedicatory Epistle

To the directors of the India Company among the Dutch, most excellent in virtue, piety, and prudence: I wish you health and happiness from God the Father and from our Lord Jesus Christ.

Most excellent lords,

Will all of sound mind not judge those who rejected ἐμπορίαν or trade as a vulgar matter unworthy of the free man to have strayed very far from all reason? Indeed, even among all the arts that may furnish and enrich a well-ordered republic, trade reaps much praise because nothing is more useful, pleasant, and honorable for a republic.[1]

Trade, however, preserves human life and supplies clothing and nourishment for oneself, as well as one's wife, children, and anyone else we hold dear and ought to protect.[2] And just as by the art of medicine the sick are provided with their needs so as to be cured of illness, so

---

[1] [The first paragraph and several other sections of this foreword are based on Petrus Landry's preface to his *De mercatura decisiones, et tractatus varii, et de rebus ad eam pertinentibus. In quibus omnium authorum, praecipue Benvenuti Stracchae* (Lyon, 1592).]

[2] [This sentence relies on Cicero, *De officiis* 1.4.12.]

by the practice of trade all people are taken care of in terms of what is of particular use to them and what is necessary to live a good life.³

Although many different perils have indeed attached themselves to trade, by importing various goods it succeeds better in raising the mind to enjoyment than its dangers manage to drag the mind down to disdain it. Now we are accustomed to admire the manifold yield from the fatherland, for which reason we also joyfully sing the praises of God's goodness to us, as indeed we ought. But how much more are we drawn to this duty of piety by the very favor of trade, by which more things are exposed to our eyes and offered to our use than the soil of our fatherland bestows on us? For no region, province, or state is self-sufficient in every respect, but the one needs the riches and assistance of the other.⁴ The one abounds in fruit, while the other abounds in gold, silver, other metals, and whatever else. As the poet elegantly puts it, "India sends her ivory, the soft Sabaeans their frankincense; but the naked Chalybes give us iron, Pontus the strong-smelling beaver's oil, and Epirus the Olympian victories of her mares."⁵

Hence it is inevitable that just as the mind of Emperor Titus was struck by the manifold splendor of the temple of Jerusalem and drawn to the greatest admiration,⁶ so also the minds of Christians will be affected by admiration and the greatest joy due to the manifold wealth of all merchandise and imported goods.

This explains why many wise and distinguished men have considered nothing more honorable than the pursuit of commerce. It is indeed true that some men confined trade within strict limits and did not allow it at all due to their excessive delight in either sluggish idleness or frightful arms. Nevertheless, the praise and reward they

---

3 [The comparison between commerce and medicine can also be found in Seneca, *De beneficiis* 4.13.]

4 [This and the following lines from Virgil are taken from Benvenuto Straccha, *Tractatus de mercatura seu mercatore*, as included in Landry, *De mercatura decisiones*, 389. They can also be found in Lilius Gregorius Gyraldus, *De re nautica libellus* (Basel, 1540), 9.]

5 [Virgil, *Georgica* 57–59; LCL 63:103.]

6 [Cf. Josephus, *De bello iudaico* 6.260.]

reaped from this is most evident in that they were best known among the other nations for their barbarity and boorishness. But people of all nations assigned the highest value to trade, and the greater their renown (as Herodotus testifies about the Greeks),[7] the more they engaged in business. In fact trade was esteemed so highly that even their wise men and philosophers did not spurn its practice.

Plutarch thus reports how Solon as a young man turned to trade.[8] Others tell us that Thales and the mathematician Hippocrates engaged in trade. So, too, it is said of many kings and princes that they devoted themselves to this art. Emperor Pertinax (as Herodian testifies)[9] practiced trade like a private citizen. And as Bodin writes in book 6 of the *Republic*,[10] does not everybody know that the kings of Portugal exercised an extensive and most lucrative trade without affront to the republic but rather to its greatest advantage? For, when in 1475 they opened the wealth of the East and India's remotest areas, together with all naval ports, to their sailors, they brought back to Portugal the truly admirable histories of those peoples and their incredible riches. Later on, they even filled all of Europe with this variety [of goods].

There are more examples of kings, but it would take too long to list the leading and private men who by the zeal devoted to trade accumulated the greatest honor and praise. What remains is to address myself to you, most excellent lords, as men who not only gained great honor among our countrymen by the trade and business you conduct in India, but have also brought it about by your business dealings that the names "Hollanders" and "Zeelanders" (that is, the bravest Dutch) represent the greatest pinnacle of honor among foreign nations. To this I add that the Indians themselves most highly approve of the way you conduct your business, for by their own experience they know that

---

[7] [This cannot be found in Herodotus, *Historiae*.]

[8] [Plutarch, *Solon* 2. This and the following lines are taken from Straccha, *Tractatus de mercatura*, in Landry, *De mercatura decisiones*, 387.]

[9] [Possibly in *Historiae de imperio* 2.4. We find the same statement in Giovanni Gioviano Pontano, *De liberalitate* (Napels, 1498), 344v. It probably refers to *Historia Augusta: Helvetius Pertinax* 13.4.]

[10] [Jean Bodin, *De republica* (Paris, 1576), 650.]

you do not act deceitfully and fraudulently, but rather do everything in good faith and without any fraud.[11] This is why they never stop singing the praises of the conduct of the Dutch merchants more than that of their counterparts from other nations.

In order that the way you conduct your business might be diligently adopted by all the merchants in Europe, I thought it would not be altogether useless in this work, with some words not of my own, but of others, to describe in detail the chief duties of piety necessary in conducting business, namely, what things should be avoided and what is useful. Indeed, for the things I offer here I have drawn on many writers, and in particular the most fertile meadows of the sacred writings. After the example of the Phrygians I have woven a single tapestry, as it were, to give my writing not so much some color as some warmth and, as it were, some spirit and life. What remains is for me, after the custom of the Athenians and Romans, to acquire προστάτας [champions] and patrons and to choose my advocates. And is there a more prudent choice for my patrons than you, most excellent lords, lovers of equity and dutiful conduct? For this reason, I turn to you in order to offer these labors of mine, however insignificant they may be, and to disseminate them under the auspices of your names. Accept this dedication as the sure τεκμήριον [proof] of a devoted mind. If so, believe me, you will be given a mind prepared for greater things. Be strong in the Lord of Hosts, most excellent men.

Kampen, 18 March 1615, in my study.
The most devoted and dedicated servant of your dignity,
Daniel Sauterius

---

[11] [This sentence relies on Cicero, *De officiis* 3.17.70.]

Preface

Before I embark on the journey I propose to take, I will begin with these words of the Apostle: "For the grace of God has appeared, bringing salvation for all people, training us to renounce ungodliness and worldly passions, and to live self-controlled, upright, and godly lives in the present age."[1]

The duties of piety required of a merchant are the following:

1. To acquire the good testimony of a good conscience.
2. To exclude all pretense and deceit from every act.
3. To pursue the integrity of honesty by avoiding all fraud.
4. To pursue with zeal the duties of justice (which renders everyone his due).
5. To refrain from exalting oneself with riches, but to pursue humility of mind as if it were a medicine best suited to all.
6. To show kindness to the poor.
7. To eradicate the evil of greed.
8. To cut off all destructive thorns of worry.
9. To despise the love of earthly things and to strive for heavenly things.

---

[1] Titus 2:11.

Our present age demands that I write some things about the duties of piety. "Come on then, let us earnestly pursue our studies, lest we use the laziness of someone else to excuse our own. There are people who hear and people who read. My only task is to elaborate something that is worth the hearing and the paper."[2] "And this not by means of my own counsel, but by that of the ancients, and even in their very words. You are my leader, great God; and direct my hand and mind, so that I may see that which is beneficial, determine it, and bring it forth."[3] Amen.

---

[2] Pliny the Younger, *Epistulae* 4.16 [LCL 55:326].

[3] Lipsius, *Politica* 1.1 [Waszink, 261].

The Cause, Matter, and Form of This Work

1. *The cause, matter, and form of this work.*

I have always admired the teaching of Plato and the Stoics that "men are born for the sake of men, that they may be able mutually to help one another."[1] For they did not fail to notice that the Greatest Artist fashioned human nature in such a way that there is no one, regardless of the many gifts nature has showered on him, who does not need both "help and good advice."[2] This is why particular praise ought to be given to anyone who so conforms himself to what nature orders that he lives not just for himself but truly also for others "and makes himself useful for the rest."[3] As the Apostle says, "Let each of you look out not only for his own interests, but also for the interests of others."[4]

Even though one might devote oneself to many different kinds of study, the wisest person judges the study that teaches human minds to live piously to be the most outstanding. "For nothing can be so outstanding or so suitable to a person than to instruct people unto

---

[1] Cicero, *De officiis* 1.22 [LCL 30:23].
[2] Plautus, *Pseudolus* 19 [LCL 260:245].
[3] Seneca, [*De otio* 3.5; LCL 254:187].
[4] Phil. 2:4.

justice."[5] And since living well applies to everyone, "the person who imparts the science of speaking well does not merit so much from human affairs as he who teaches to live piously and innocently."[6] This is why Cicero, that unrivalled parent of the Latin language, says that he "would rather have only one small book by which people are incited to cultivate virtues than a polished oration in behalf of a seditious man."[7] He pronounced this view since he believed that the best and most profitable thing philosophy can give is precepts for living. "If those to whom the truth is not known do this, how much more should we do it who have been enlightened and instructed by God?"[8] Let us therefore do our best to offer something "for the profit of our readers, if not for eloquence (because there is in me but a slight stream of eloquence) then at any rate for living."[9]

My design is to prescribe some duties of piety for the merchants of the present age, so that they may be incited all the more to conduct their business in an upright manner and be directed to perfect and accomplish the way of piety. "For in my opinion piety is the basis of all virtues."[10] And, as that teacher of the gentiles says, "Godliness is profitable for all things, having promise of the life that now is and of that which is to come."[11] To this end, so that the merchant might be guided to the safe haven of his salvation, as it were, I will—to the extent that my mediocre mind permits it—strive "to bring maxims together, beautiful maxims, sharp maxims, and, may salvation bestow

---

[5] Lactantius, *De vero cultu* [*Divinarum institutionum libri VII*] 6.2 [FC 49:395].

[6] Lactantius, *De falsa religione* [*Divinarum institutionum libri VII*] 1.1 [FC 49:16].

[7] Cicero, *Hortensius* [frag. 47; quoted in Lactantius, *Divinarum institutionum libri VII* 6.2; FC 49:395].

[8] Lactantius, *De vero cultu* [*Divinarum institutionum libri VII*] 6.2 [FC 49:395].

[9] Lactantius, *De opificio Dei* 21 [FC 54:56].

[10] Cicero, *Pro Plancio* 29.12 [LCL 158:443].

[11] 1 Tim. 4:8.

this upon me, conceived for the salvation of humankind."[12] Since we know that whatever is of received authority is of greater weight, I wish to make an elegant patchwork quilt of maxims to emulate bees rather than spiders. "For the spider's web [*textus*] is woven while it spins from its own entrails; our text will not be such."[13] Bees, by contrast, settle on glittering and sparkling flowers of all colors. They "sip all sweets in the flowery glades,"[14] and their only goal is to "pack the fluid honey and strain their cells to bursting with sweet nectar."[15] Let me therefore pluck the most exquisite little flowers from the books of different writers as if they were the charming meadows and gardens of others and offer you profitable and pleasant libations from them. "I seem to be promising a great thing, but there is need of the help of heaven so that opportunity and time be granted me for achieving this aim."[16] It is my prayer that the most merciful Lord God will make "my labor direct some men whom it has freed from their errors toward the path of heaven."[17]

---

[12] Lipsius, *Politica*, preface [Waszink, 232].

[13] Lipsius, [*notae* to *Politica* 1; Waszink, 722].

[14] Lucretius, [*De rerum natura*] 3 [LCL 181:189].

[15] Virgil, [*Aeneid* 1.442–43; LCL 63:293].

[16] Lactantius, *De opificio Dei* 21 [=20; FC 54:56].

[17] Ibid.

1

Acquire the Testimony of a Good Conscience

2. The first duty of piety is that the merchant should be concerned with an upright conscience, which is to be valued more highly than empty glory.

Most true indeed is the view expressed by a man who did not know the Christian religion: "Narrow are the bounds within which nature has confined our lives, but those of our fame are infinite."[1] For we all are drawn to the pursuit of praise, and every person of good standing is mainly guided by fame. But no one is more dangerous or dishonorable than he whose soul is incited to sin by the hope of earthly fame. Do you see how they conduct themselves in the crowd and on the marketplace today? Indeed, "many fear their reputation, few their conscience."[2]

Not so for the good man, however. He casts off the desire for false fame and an empty reputation in conducting business and strives to maintain the good testimony of his conscience (which is indeed the merchant's great duty of piety), so that he can frankly say at all times and before all people, "our boasting is this: the testimony of our conscience."[3] We should guard against the desire for the empty fame that does not have the conscience as its companion. What is the

---

[1] Cicero, *Pro Rabirio Perduellionis Reo* [10.30; LCL 198:485].

[2] Pliny the Younger, *Epistulae* 3.20 [LCL 55:235].

[3] 2 Cor. 1:12.

difference? "The empty fame of this age is deceiving."[4] More than that, "it is most base! That is why the tragic poet was not wrong when he exclaimed: 'Fame, in myriads of mortals, is nothing other than the great puffing up of their ears.'"[5] How great is earthly fame? "Destroy ambition, it is a swollen, idle, and empty thing."[6] If only it did not incite to wicked acts! For it easily tears from the minds the equity "in whose defense a magnanimous man should stake everything."[7] And "those whom it holds captive it easily moves to all manner of sin so that they do what they think will earn them admiration, regardless of how repulsive or dishonorable it may be. So it not only upsets all honorable acts, but also travels to the wicked."[8]

Do you want me to say a lot about these few things? "Thirst for fame and longing for renown allow nothing to seem inaccessible, nothing remote."[9] Consider, on the contrary, what a good conscience does. It sings a sweet and gentle song to its Lord: "Live so as to please God."[10] It declares, "For a good man, it is unseemly ever to deviate from the truth in the slightest, or to inflict any unjust loss on anyone, or to be involved in any kind of fraudulent activity."[11] Nothing should therefore be done for the sake of empty fame. Everything ought rather to be done by the dictate and guidance of the conscience, and all ought

---

[4] Augustine, *Enarrationes in Psalmos* [taken from Joseph Lang, *Loci communes sive Florilegium rerum et materiarum selectarum* (Strasbourg, 1605), 258v (s.v. *gloria*); it could not be traced to Augustine].

[5] Boethius, *De consolatione philosophiae* 3.6 [LCL 74:253–55].

[6] Seneca, [*Epistulae morales* 84.11; LCL 76:283].

[7] Cicero, *De officiis* 1.68 [LCL 30:71].

[8] [Pseudo-]Basil of Caesarea, *Constitutiones monasticae*, ch. 11 [probably taken from Thomas Stapleton, *Promptuarium morale ... Pars hyemalis* (Antwerp, 1593), 182].

[9] Quintus Curtius, [*Historiae Alexandri Magni* 9.2.9; LCL 369:377].

[10] Nicolas Reusner, *Symbolorum* [*imperatorium. Classica prima* (Frankfort, 1588), 278].

[11] Ambrose, *De officiis ministrorum* 1.73 [Davidson, 399].

to have it impressed on them that they "not stray a hairbreadth from the path of conscience in any part of life."[12]

3. The good things of a good conscience: their magnitude and kind.

Is there anyone who fails to see that an upright conscience is better than fame? For when people neglect their conscience and only have eyes for their reputation, they fail to pursue the fame that is lasting and true. For true fame "strikes deep root and spreads its branches wide."[13] There can be no true fame without a good conscience, and so no right-thinking person ever elevates his fame above the conscience. When that instrument of God wanted true fame, how did he try to obtain it? "In this," he says, "I myself always strive to have a conscience without offense toward God and men."[14] What value did the Roman Sage attach to conscience? He valued it so highly "that no one seemed to rate virtue higher or was more consecrated to virtue than he who had lost his reputation as a good man in order to keep from losing the approval of his conscience."[15] For fame can often disappoint, but conscience never does. This is why the fame and mark of one who has been born again, if indeed he is pervaded by the spirit, is "life and peace to the conscience."[16]

There is a spacious theater for this virtue, in which its fame flourishes abundantly, [and] brings delight to its witnesses and panegyrists. Rightly he says, "There is no greater theater for virtue than the conscience."[17] The more one nourishes it within, the greater the fame with which one lives! "To the one whose conscience testifies throughout his life to good deeds, he will live wholly fearless."[18] For the mind

---

[12] Cicero, *Epistulae ad Atticum* 13 [LCL 491:89].

[13] Cicero, *De officiis* 2.43 [LCL 30:211–13].

[14] Acts 24:16.

[15] Seneca, *Epistulae morales* 81.21 [LCL 76:233].

[16] Rom. 8:6.

[17] Cicero, *Tusculanae disputationes* 2.64 [LCL 141:219].

[18] Cicero, *Pro Cluentio* 159 [LCL 198:397].

with good conscience "is always free of fear."[19] He lives with honor, since the strength of an upright man is "the confidence of a trustworthy conscience; his majesty, the splendor of a good reputation."[20] He lives in joy, since "in a human the happiness of a good conscience is a paradise. Therefore, do you never want to be sad? Then live well. An untroubled mind bears sadness with ease. A good life always has joy."[21] That man dies in peace, for "a good conscience gives comfort to the dying and lasts forever."[22] Can anyone therefore imagine any greater blessing than the treasure of a good conscience in all his actions? "Let this be our wall of bronze: to have no guilt at heart, no wrongdoing to turn us pale."[23] "It has its adornment in greatness of mind, which cares nothing for show but refers everything to conscience."[24] "Blessed is he whose conscience does not condemn him, and who is not fallen from his hope in the Lord."[25]

---

[19] Bias, in Stobaeus, [*Florilegium*] 3.24.11 [probably taken from Lipsius, *Politica* 1.5; Waszink, 278].

[20] Bernard of Clairvaux, *Sermones* [actually *De consideratione* 3.14; CF 37:97].

[21] Augustine, *De catechumenis*. [The first part of the quote ("In homine ... laetitia paradisus est") is actually from *De Genesi ad litteram* 12.34 (WSA 1/13:503), as Souterius's source, Simon Goulart, *Apophthegmatum sacrorum loci communes* (s.l., 1592), 58, acknowledges, but Goulart erroneously links it to the next one from *De catechumenis*. Souterius quite likely took the second part of the quote, beginning at "vis nunquam," from Lang, *Loci communes*, 123v (s.v. *conscientia*), where it is attributed to Isidore, *Soliloquies* 2.]

[22] [Pseudo-]Bernard of Clairvaux, *De conscientia* [from Goulartius, *Apophthegmatum*, 58].

[23] Horace, *Epistulae* 1.1 [LCL 194:255].

[24] Pliny the Younger, *Epistulae* 1.22 [LCL 55:69].

[25] Sir. 14:2.

4. Refutation of those who attach greater value to fame based on wealth gained unfairly than to a right conscience.

At this point we need to refute the error of those who, when they grow rich by wicked merchant practices and unfair means, convince themselves that they are rising to the summit of fame and to the highest rank, or even think that they have already achieved that height when they see that they, "like Nicias the Athenian, have reached the greatest dignity because of their wealth,"[26] or when they think that this wealth has made them noble, "just as riches ennobled Simon the Athenian."[27] This view seizes them in particular when they notice that they are receiving distinctions from the people and are proudly greeted as rich men by those they meet on the street. Eager as they are for honors, and preferring the approval of the people above all else (to the neglect of the good of a good conscience), they applaud themselves no less than the man in Thucydides who "was full of joy over a golden fish"[28] and proclaim themselves no less prosperous than "the fisherman Gripus when he had recovered the trunk from the sea."[29]

Consider, however, that their fame and felicity is in no way real. For they have paved their way to this fame through the troubles of others and the calamities of their neighbors. Therefore, if they want to be truly felicitous and enjoy true fame, they would be better off "to go back home."[30] That is to say, if they were to restore to each what they have gained with wicked trickery, "they would be thrown into

---

[26] Plutarch, *Nicias* [15; LCL 65:261–63].

[27] Plutarch [*Moralia* 776B, which briefly alludes to Simon, a cobbler; LCL 321:29].

[28] Thucydides. [Perhaps Souterius had in mind the dream of the golden fish described in Theocritus, *Idylls*, 21; LCL 28:283–89.]

[29] See Plautus, *Rudens*, lines 906–37 [LCL 260:497–89. Upon hauling a trunk from the sea with his net, the fisherman Gripus counts himself happy, thinking he can buy his freedom—only to discover that it contains toys.]

[30] Juan Luis Vives, commentary on Augustine, *De civitate Dei* 2.21 [Vives refers to Lactantius, who wrote that Carneades had observed that if the Romans would restitute their unjustly acquired wealth, they would languish

need and misery,"³¹ "since wealth sought for its own sake and at any cost cannot be expedient if linked with shame."³² Moreover, what fame is left to them if it involves crime? Any fame sought in words of the people rather than from fact can never be true, not even when it does come from deeds but still "involves crime, in which there can be no fame."³³ But what if this external honor was given to them? If there is no inner peace of conscience, "a guilty conscience cannot draw on hope."³⁴ "Therefore, those who are being punished always bear their guilt in their conscience. Their guilty mind is never free of cares; rather, the mind with a guilty conscience is always troubled by its own torments."³⁵ This is why we should say, "What use is it if all people sing praises but the conscience accuses?"³⁶

I ask them, Do you think fame is sound when it begins by opening the door to the greatest sins and vices and continues by putting all remaining virtues to death? For "empty fame is a thief of spiritual wealth, a flattering enemy of souls, a moth to virtues; under its honey-coated deceit, it offers its poisons and holds out its deadly cup."³⁷ Consider also how narrowly and strictly confined the possession of fame is, and also how trifling and meagre. "For the fame of riches is fleeting."³⁸ Those whom it arouses by its charms are mocked by a

---

in poverty and primitive huts again. See Augustine, *De civitate Dei, libri xxii*, ed. Juan Luis Vives (Antwerp, 1600), 359.]

³¹ Lactantius, *De iustitia* [*Divinarum institutionum libri VII*] 5.1 [FC 49:367].

³² Cicero, *De officiis* 3.87 [LCL 30:361; trans. note: I read *expetūtur* (=*expetuntur*) for *expetitur*].

³³ Ibid.

³⁴ Augustine, *Sermones*. [This seems to be a paraphrase of *Enarrationes in Psalmos*, 31.2.5.]

³⁵ Isidore, *Soliloquies* 2.61 [MPL 83:859].

³⁶ Gregory, *Homiliae XL in Ezechielem* 1.9.15 [MPL 76:876].

³⁷ [Pseudo-]Basil of Caesarea, *Constitutiones monasticae* 11 [probably from Stapleton, *Promptuarium morale ... Pars hyemalis*, 182].

³⁸ Sallust, *De coniuratione Catilinae* 1 [LCL 116:21].

false slumber, as it were, only to leave them thereafter. "Therefore, despise all these things that have only the semblance of fame, deriving from meaningless badges of distinction; hold them for brief, unreal, perishable things."[39] You will never be right to call a merchant full of glory who by a multitude of sins and the most repulsive deception is seeking after the people's favor and ear. "One would not be right to call happy the man of many possessions; the title of happy is more rightly claimed by the man"[40] who applies his mind to a right conscience and holds the renown and vapor of earthly fame in contempt.

---

[39] Cicero, *Epistulae ad familiares* 377 [LCL 230:47].
[40] Horace, *Carmina* 4.9 [LCL 33:247].

2

Exclude All Pretense and Deceit

5. The second duty of piety that the merchant ought to pursue is to exclude[1] from every act all pretense and deceit.

In the speech he delivered in defense of Ctesiphon, Demosthenes calls Aeschines a tragic ape "because, although an utter rascal, he used splendid language to act the part of an upright citizen."[2] O how I wish that this taunting expression could not be applied to so many others! "Any of those who use their personal appearance to parade their pursuit of wisdom can easily be compared with this man."[3] The same applies to those who, in order to dupe others in their many sales, purchases, and trades, "have one thought locked in their breast, another ready on their tongue, and prefer to show a good front rather than a good heart."[4] Indeed, "so ready is pretense in the human heart"[5] for profit that, although they wish to be considered "in countenance and character a man of the old school and stern in the judgment of what

---

[1] [Trans. note: I read *secludere* for *secludente*.]

[2] Demosthenes, *De corona* 242 [taken from Erasmus, *Adagia*, 2.8.95; CWE 34:87].

[3] Pliny the Younger, *Epistulae* 1.12 [LCL 55:69].

[4] Sallust, *Demosthenes* 10 [LCL 116:35].

[5] Quintus Curtius, [*Historiae Alexandri Magni*] 5.10.13 [LCL 368:405].

is right,"[6] nevertheless they are deceitful, and whatever they do, they do it with pretense and deceit. My fervent wish is for the merchant to be different. For could there be anything more repulsive than for him in his business dealings to be otherwise affected in mind than his words and looks suggest? "Pretense and deceit should be done away with in all departments of our daily life. Then an honest man will not be guilty of either pretense or deceit in order to buy or to sell to better advantage."[7] What Emperor Frederick III observed about his counselors you can rightly apply to merchants: "Would that they left two things behind in the forecourt of the marketplace: pretense and deceit! For thus they would counsel rightly"[8] and the traders' republic would be blessed. So, too, "it is characteristic of the good man, who might also be called the wise man, to maintain this first rule in friendship: let there be no feigning or pretense."[9] This is not something that ought to be remembered in friendship alone, but in every business undertaking—especially since pretense or deceit is always accompanied by evil fraud, "because criminal fraud consists in false pretense."[10] Therefore, whoever acts deceivingly also acts fraudulently. But what could be more becoming of a Christian than to see to it that there is no fraud in him and that his dealings remain undefiled by any vice of pretense and deceit? The others I will not count among the wise and those endowed with true wisdom: for to trip someone slyly or to strip him deceitfully "is not wisdom descending from above, but is earthly, sensual, and demonic."[11] True wisdom, which is also "from above,"

---

[6] Tacitus, *Historiae* 1.14 [LCL 111:27].

[7] Cicero, *De officiis* 3.60 [LCL 30:331].

[8] Aeneas Sylvius Piccolomini, *In libros Antonii Panormitae ... Commentarius* [(Basel, 1538), 213], on Panormita, *De dictis et factis Alphonsi regis Aragonum* 3.2. [For this joke, see *One Hundred Renaissance Jokes: An Anthology*, ed. Barbara C. Bowen (Birmingham: Summa, 1988), 13.]

[9] Cicero, *De amicitia* 18 [LCL 154:177].

[10] Cicero, *De officiis* 3.61 [LCL 30:331].

[11] James 3:15.

is "without pretense."[12] It is straightforward and candid. "It does not think one thing when it stands, another when it sits."[13] "Therefore, who is wise and understanding among you? Let him show by good conduct that his works are done in the meekness of wisdom."[14]

6. The necessity of putting off pretense and deceit as required by integrity.

Every Christian (if he is at least endowed with natural knowledge) should know whether it is possible to hide something from God and men. "Yet we still should do nothing that savors of greed or of injustice, of lust or of intemperance."[15] "For we are born for integrity."[16] He who pursues this integrity will readily prefer a forthright mind over pretense and deceit (by which repulsive and unjust things are concealed). This is why, according to Cicero, Plato introduces Gyges, who found a golden ring in a cave, and "as often as he turned the bezel of the ring inward toward the palm of his hand, became invisible to everyone, while he himself saw everything."[17] (A similar myth is told about Pluto's helmet.) But to return to Gyges: "As often as he turned the ring back to its proper position, he became visible again. And so he used the advantage the ring gave him."[18] He committed many crimes, "but no one was able to detect him in his crimes. Thus, by virtue of the ring, he shortly rose to be king of Lydia."[19] But, when the wise men were asked "whether, if a wise man had just such a ring, he would imagine that he was freer to do wrong than if he did not have

---

[12] James 3:17.

[13] [Pseudo-]Sallust, *Invectiva in Ciceronem* 7 [LCL 462:371].

[14] James 3:13.

[15] Cicero, *De officiis* 3.37 [LCL 30:305].

[16] Cicero, *De officiis* 3.36 [LCL 30:303].

[17] Cicero, *De officiis* 3.38 [LCL 30:305]; Plato, *Laws* 10 [actually *Republic* 360A].

[18] Cicero, *De officiis* 3.38 [LCL 30:305–7].

[19] Cicero, *De officiis* 3.38 [LCL 30:307].

it,"[20] they said this could not be, "since good men do not aim to secure secrecy but the right."[21] "Moreover, integrity is not to be sacrificed to some considerable advantage."[22]

But suppose I were to ask a Christian, "If nobody were to know or even to suspect the truth when you do anything to gain riches or power or sovereignty—if your act should be hidden forever from the knowledge of God and men, would you do it?"[23] How much more will he deny this who holds integrity in such high esteem, that no cause intervenes that is powerful enough to confuse his mind with the appearance and expectation of profit? Instead, let this heroic motto be impressed upon his mind: "It is better to die than to act against virtue and equity."[24] For that reason, we ought to be candid and forthright. Of them it ought to be truly clear "who bear a ready mind upon their brow."[25] For the great virtue that philosophers, orators, and the popular voices of Christians equally celebrate with the highest praises is a candid heart, "plain and unvarnished."[26]

7. The necessity of excluding all pretense and deceit is further inferred from the vision of God which is directed at all human actions.

The above teaching of a philosopher who had only been illuminated by the natural light has been left to us in writing, but it is impressed upon us even more powerfully by that divine teacher Paul when he urges us to leave behind works of darkness and to put on the armor of light so as "to walk with integrity, as in the day."[27] For when the

---

[20] Ibid.

[21] Ibid.

[22] Ibid.

[23] Ibid.

[24] Aristotle, *Ethica nichomachea* 3 [Reference not found; however, the same source is mentioned in, for example, Domenico Nani Mirabelli, *Polyanthea opus suavissimis floribus exornatum* (Cologne, 1552), 297 (s.v. *virtus*).]

[25] Aulus Gellius, [*Noctes atticae* 19.8; LCL 212:373].

[26] Cicero, *Epistulae ad Atticum* 1.1 [LCL 7:49].

[27] Rom. 13:13.

apostle fills our ears with such words he wants the purest life to be not only inscribed on our hearts, but also to be rendered visible in all our senses, acts, and outward works, persuading us that we can do nothing that God, "in whose sight we live, does not see."[28] He is the examiner of our works. "Him, viewing all things from his height, no mass of earth obstructs."[29] He discerns what is open, and knows what is hidden. "There really is a God who hears and sees what we are doing. The man who deserves good, he will reward well; the man who deserves ill, he will treat in the same way."[30] "Since he alone sees all things, you could call him the true sun."[31] This Augustine indicated in a fitting way when he admonished some scoundrel in the presence of the people as follows: "If you want to sin, of course, find somewhere he cannot see you, and then do what you like. For if you do evil where God does not see you, you will have your reward."[32] It is as if he is saying, "So it is not possible in any way to evade the eyes of God."[33] "Anyone who has a sinful heart never escapes notice; in the end he is assuredly revealed, who was previously hidden."[34]

Let us use this knowledge to form a judgment on mores and lifestyles. For there is no one who should not fear the sight of God. Yet how does he do so properly? By reminding himself that "we are open to God. Therefore, there is no place for lying, no place for dissimulation."[35] Indeed, that care ought to be there in the mind of the Christian, who is called to "walk before God forever."[36] "Yet in the presence of even

---

[28] Lactantius, *De vero cultu* [*Divinarum institutionum libri VII*] 6.24 [FC 49:464].

[29] Boethius, [*De consolatione philosophiae*] 5.2 [LCL 74:393].

[30] Plautus, *Captivi* [313–15; LCL 60:539].

[31] Boethius, [*De consolatione philosophiae*] 5.2 [LCL 74:395].

[32] Augustine, [*Sermones ad populum* 132.3.3; WSA 3/4:327].

[33] Hesiod, *Opera et dies* 105 [LCL 57:95].

[34] Solon, [*Elegia* 13.26–27; LCL 258:131].

[35] Lactantius, *De vero cultu* [*Divinarum institutionum libri VII*] 6.24 [FC 49:465].

[36] Gen. 17:1.

an image of God you would not dare to do any of the things you are now doing. But when God himself is present within you, seeing and hearing everything, are you not ashamed to be doing such things as these, O you who are insensible of your own nature, and object of God's wrath!"[37]

8. The necessity of doing nothing with pretense or deceit is demonstrated from God's intervention in human thoughts as well.

I will admit that the human mind[38] is rather rash in all it does with pretense and deceit, since people all too often hope that what they do will remain unknown to others. But of what use is that? "Even if we are able to hide from all men, we cannot shut out God, to whom nothing can be hidden, nothing secret."[39] For this reason, when someone asked the philosopher Thales "whether a man could hide an evil deed from the gods,"[40] he answered both wisely and truly: "Not even an evil thought." "Also the secrets of this mind lie open to the divinity."[41] "He is witness of our souls, and he comes into the very midst of our thoughts."[42] "There is no advantage in having a closed up conscience; we are open to God."[43] For that reason, we ought to have not only pure hands, but also a pure mind, and to seek nothing more than to have a spirit that is free from the evil of pretense and deceit. "Let us, then, cleanse our conscience, which is pervious to the eyes of God, and let us always so live as if we thought we were to render an account. And let

---

[37] Arrian, *Epicteti Dissertationes* 2.8.14 [LCL 131:257].

[38] [Trans. note: I read *hominis* for *hominus*.]

[39] Lactantius, *De vero cultu* [*Divinarum institutionum libri VII*] 6.24 [FC 49:494].

[40] Thales in Diogenes Laertius, [*Vitae philosophorum* 1.1.36; LCL 184:37; the margin also includes a reference to Cicero, *De legibus* 2, but this seems to be an error].

[41] Lactantius, *De ira Dei* 24 [FC 54:116].

[42] Seneca, *Epistulae morales* 83.1 [LCL 76:259].

[43] Lactantius, *De vero cultu* [*Divinarum institutionum libri VII*] 6.24 [FC 49:465].

us think that at every moment we are not in some theater of this world watched by men, but that we are being observed from above by him who will be both judge and witness. Nor will it be permitted anyone to deny his deed to him when he demands an account of our lives."[44]

9. The necessity of destroying pretense and deceit finally is deduced from the fact that God's divinity sees and knows the whole man.

Finally, O merchant, you would no doubt do well to set and keep before your eyes a Guardian of whom you are mindful, believing that he sees your entire being. Would it not be to your honor if you acted as if you lived in the sight of a good and always present Prince? Where people do not live this way, they soon turn to wickedness and malice, "since solitude prompts us to all kinds of evil."[45] But would you not gain even greater honor and profit if you lived in the sight of a God who perceives all things from above? Anyone who circumscribes himself in this way with the authority of a living God will be sure to keep himself from the sin of pretense and deceit. For "by the intervention of the majesty of God, a wise man soon learns to keep his vices in check."[46] "No man will readily sin if he considers God everywhere present with him."[47] "For conscience greatly checks men, if we believe that we are living in the sight of God; if we realize that not only what we do is seen from above, but also that what we think or say is heard by God."[48] This is why the apostle warns, "Let everyone turn away from evil and do good; let him seek peace and pursue it."[49] The reason he adds is this: "For the eyes of the Lord are on the righteous, and his ears are open to their prayers; but the face of the Lord is against those who do evil."[50] "There remains also as an observer from on high foreknowing

---

[44] Ibid.

[45] Seneca, *Epistulae morales* 25.5 [LCL 75:185].

[46] Seneca [loosely quoted from *Epistulae morales* 25.6; LCL 75:187].

[47] Clement of Alexandria, [*Paedagogus* 3.5; FC 23:227].

[48] Lactantius, *De ira Dei* 8 [FC 54:74].

[49] 1 Peter 3:11.

[50] 1 Peter 3:12.

all things, God, and the always present eternity of his sight runs along with the future quality of our actions dispensing rewards for the good and punishments for the wicked. Turn away then from vices, cultivate virtues, lift up your mind to righteous hopes, offer up humble prayers to heaven. A great necessity is solemnly ordained for you if you do not want to deceive yourselves, to do good, when you act before the eyes of a judge who sees all things."[51] Therefore, O merchant, whoever you may be, "live as if in plain sight of God."[52] Think as if someone "could look into our inmost souls."[53] Speak with others "as if God is listening."[54] Conduct your business as one who one day "will give an account of your stewardship."[55] If you put your mind to these things, you will not try to beguile, cheat, or defraud anyone in your buying and selling.

---

[51] Boethius, [*De consolatione philosophiae* 5.6; LCL 74:433–35].

[52] Seneca, *Epistulae morales* 83.1 [LCL 76:259].

[53] Seneca, *De moribus* [actually from Seneca, *Epistulae morales* 83.1; LCL 76:259].

[54] Tertullian, *Apologeticum* 39 [could not be found].

[55] Luke 16:2.

3

Pursue the Integrity of Honesty by Avoiding Fraud

10. The third duty of piety to which the merchant ought to apply himself is to avoid fraud and to pursue a complete honesty in everything. First, the word "fraud."

Fraud, too, is to be abolished from all business. To me "fraud" means "a crafty and wicked plan deviating from virtue and truth as well as the laws of honesty."[1] This is why it is a mistake when some people call "prudence" that which deceives under the appearance and semblance of virtue, seeming all the more useful to them the greater its shrewdness. "For admiring shrewd and crafty men, they take cunning for wisdom. But they must be disabused of this error and their way of thinking must be wholly converted to the understanding that they can obtain what they desire only by upright plans and just acts, and not by cheating and cunning."[2] How can the fraudulent action of a crafty merchant be wisdom or prudence when by it "truth is covered with deceiving practices aiming at one's own advantage"?[3] The fact of the matter is that fraud is far removed from truth, and "a double

---

[1] George Thomson, *Vindex veritatis adversus Iustum Lipsium* [(London, 1606), 38].

[2] Cicero, *De officiis* 2.10 [LCL 30:179].

[3] [Pseudo-]Augustine, *De definitionibus* [taken from Lang, *Loci communes*, 249r (s.v. *fraus*)].

diapason apart,"4 "since the function of prudence is to choose the good."5 Deceitfulness, by way of contrast, aims at every injustice and at the disadvantage of one's neighbor; it prefers wicked acts over good, urges the mind to cheat with every crooked desire, and so "rather merits the name of fraudulent profligacy and cunning."6 They therefore have no ground to give their vices beautiful names and "[to be led] by their greed to translate their very vices into virtues."7 But enough about the term. Yet we did think it necessary to begin this way, since we want to be merchants who are neither cheaters nor "masters of harm and wickedness."8 Instead, we want to be "courageous and high-souled men, and at the same time good and straightforward, lovers of truth, and foes to deception."9

11. *Fraud and honesty compared, so that the former's repulsive nature and the latter's excellence become manifest.*

What, I ask, does a Christian merchant have to do with fraud? "No self-interest will ever drive the good into fraud, while the bad are often impelled thereto by one that is but trivial."10 The longing of the bad is to be detested and the mindset of the good praised. "Consider every detail, and examine it for yourself."11 You will see how great a difference separates the two. The poet wrote these well-known words: "By cheating virtue is vanquished."12 This is why the more craftily and cunningly someone cheats, the more hated he is "and the more

---

4 Erasmus, *Adagia*, 1.2.63 [CWE 31:202].

5 Cicero, *De officiis* 3.17 [LCL 30:341].

6 Ibid. [Reference could not be found. Souterius seems to be paraphrasing Cicero, *De officiis* 1.19; LCL 30:65.]

7 Tacitus, *Historiae* 1.52 [LCL 111:91].

8 Plato [Plutarch, *Moralia* (Saying of Spartans) 220C; LCL 245:319].

9 Cicero, *De officiis* 1.63 [LCL 30:65].

10 Cicero, *Pro Milone* 12 [LCL 252:41].

11 Lucian, *Apologia* 11 [taken from Erasmus, *Adagia*, 1.2.63; CWE 31:202].

12 Ovid, *Fasti* 2.227 [LCL 253:73].

mistrusted, once his reputation for probity is taken away."[13] "Indeed, he who plots to do evil is called the worst scoundrel."[14] Moreover, he who undertakes something through deceit in vain wants God "to light an auspicious torch for him."[15] "He who has a deceitful mind will not pursue the good, and he who has a perverse tongue falls into evil."[16] Do these things seem insignificant to you? Hear then the very worst: fraud "has sent the souls of many men down to Hades."[17]

Since fraud bears so much evil within itself, we must fix our eyes on the good things that good faith brings. In fact, "there is nothing better than good faith."[18] It "strengthens friendships that grow more firm by lapse of time and binds them with chains of lasting adamant."[19] It wins great credit among the well-ordered Republic, for which we have an example in "Aratus of Sicyon, whom Antigonus treated with great intimacy because of his honesty and resolution."[20] If it is found in you, "then all will call you a just man, will follow, revere, and love you."[21] Therefore, "never behave meanly for the sake of profit."[22] "May success be lacking rather than honesty."[23] "[For] there is nothing in a merchant that burns with a brighter light than good faith."[24]

---

[13] Cicero, *De officiis* 2.34 [LCL 30:203].

[14] Prov. 24:8.

[15] Plautus, *Persae* 515 [LCL 163:515].

[16] Prov. 17:20.

[17] Homer, *Ilias* 1.3 [LCL 170:13].

[18] *Glossa in lege a procuratore c. man.* [taken from Straccha, in Landry, *De mercatura decisiones*, 388].

[19] Claudian, *De consulato Stilichonis* 2.22 [LCL 136:5].

[20] Plutarch, *Aratus* 43 [LCL 103:101].

[21] Seneca, *De quatuor virtutibus cardinalibus* [currently attributed to Martin of Braga and known as *Formula vitae honestae* 5; FC 62:94].

[22] Terence, *Hecyra* 5.3.836 [LCL 22:235].

[23] Seneca [could not be found].

[24] Straccha, [*Tractatus de mercatura*, in Landry, *De mercatura decisiones*, 388, citing Pope John II in *Codex Justinianus* 1.8.2].

12. How highly various gentiles valued honesty.

It should come as no surprise that we are urging merchants to keep to honesty and to hold it in high esteem. For very many gentiles have valued it so highly that they sought their fame in it. Cicero went so far as to boast that the Romans "excelled neither Spain in population, nor Gaul in vigor, nor Carthage in versatility, nor Greece in art, but did excel every race and every nation in good faith, piety, and religion."[25] So, too, the Arabs learned to preserve honesty "and to hold it in such high esteem that they believed human society to be erected with honesty, and had a higher regard for honesty than for profit."[26] Similarly, honesty was cultivated by the Persians, "who judged nothing to be more sacred than honesty, nothing more beautiful than silence, and nothing more disgusting than loquaciousness. They wanted to protect the first by death, and to censure the second with death."[27] It is also known "how honestly the Lapps of the north dealt with things."[28] Tacitus, too, writes that "no people in the world ranked before the Germans in arms or loyalty."[29] And, lest I conceal the merit of other nations, "the Lucanians are considered honest," and "the Milanese freely point out a thing's defects when they sell, and are honest to the point of death."[30]

Return, O Christian, to yourself, and consider what would be beautiful for you to excel in. In fraud? Perish the thought! Rather, "be honest to the honest (nay, indeed even to the dishonest!), and take care that your honesty does not fluctuate."[31] May this be your merit, the mark

---

[25] Cicero, *De haruspicum responsis* 9 [LCL 158:341].

[26] Alexander of Alexandria, [*Geniales dies* 5.10,] citing *Herod.* l. 3.

[27] Theodor Zwinger, *Theatrum humanae vitae* [(Basel, 1586), 7.4].

[28] Olaus Magnus, [*Historia de gentibus septentrionalibus* (Rome, 1555), 4.5–6 (p. 137)].

[29] Tacitus, [*Annales* 13.54; LCL 322:95].

[30] Gregorius Richterus, *Axiomata politica* [(Görlitz, 1604), 810].

[31] Plautus, *Aulularia* [*Captivi* 439; LCL 60:551].

of your life, that you deal with all "as good honesty requires, without deception."[32]

13. Acting in good faith is taught by the Greatest Lawgiver's command.

Who does not know that there ought to be a single rule for honesty and profit in business? "Indeed, nothing is really profitable that is not at the same time morally right; nothing is morally right that conflicts (with good faith)."[33] Let us therefore listen to the voice of God, the Greatest Lawgiver: "You shall neither steal, nor lie, nor deal falsely with your neighbor."[34] In these words a threefold duty is prescribed for the merchant, since (1) theft, (2) lying, and (3) deception are forbidden.

Inasmuch as theft is forbidden, people are enjoined "not to profit by their neighbor's loss,"[35] "nor to defraud or injure their neighbor to gain some personal profit."[36] For "to draw profit from the evils that befall another"[37] is a repulsive thing. Woe to anyone who prospers at the expense of another and "struts around gloating at his misfortune"![38]

Second, since the Greatest Lawgiver forbids every lie, we readily understand that "every lie must be kept entirely out of business transactions: the seller will not deceive a bidder, nor will the buyer engage one to bid [low] against himself."[39] But it is the duty of both to demand that whatever is spoken and done follows the rule of good faith; indeed, "the good strive after these things: wealth, honesty, a good reputation, fame, and friendly relations."[40]

---

[32] Cicero, *De officiis* 3.70 [LCL 30.341].

[33] Cicero, *De officiis* 3.34 [LCL 30:301].

[34] Lev. 19:11.

[35] Cicero, *De officiis* 3.21 [LCL 30:289].

[36] Cicero, *De officiis* 3.21 [LCL 30:289].

[37] Lactantius, *De vero cultu* [*Divinarum institutionum libri VII*] 6.18. [In this form, actually from Lactantius, *Epitome divinarum institutionum* 64.]

[38] Horace, *Epodi* 15 [LCL 33:307].

[39] Cicero, *De officiis* 3.61 [LCL 30:331].

[40] Plautus, *Trinummus* 272–73 [LCL 328:147].

Third, when we hear the prohibition "on dealing falsely with one's neighbor," we conclude that also in business transactions "cunning practices are to be kept out."[41] "To deceive a person is a shameful thing, and does not befit an upright man."[42] "Therefore, merchants should conduct themselves well in all their dealings, and abstain from that which is forbidden."[43]

14. Pure honesty is recommended by way of two examples.

It is part of the Christian merchant's duty to "investigate the circumstances under which commerce is lawfully (and faithfully) conducted."[44] For since among the Egyptians no one pleased King Amasis unless he lived by just gain, whence "according to the command of King Amasis anyone who lived by unfairly gained profit was punished with death."[45] How much less will the King of Kings take pleasure in anyone who uses "a Megarian trick"[46] to gain property by deception and fakery? We know that God loves the faithful, and so we ought to walk in honesty and in sincerity of mind. Why did the patriarch Jacob champion it so strongly "when he was buying the parcel of land where he had pitched his tent, from the children of Hamor, Shechem's father, for one hundred pieces of money"?[47] Because, among other reasons, he had "the sister of justice, incorruptible honesty and naked truth."[48] Why did the Lord God first reveal the birth of his Son not to the great men of

---

[41] Cicero, *De officiis* 3.71 [LCL 30.341].

[42] *Accurs. in l. semper in contract. ff. de regimis* [Straccha, *Tractatus de mercatura*, in Landry, *De mercatura decisiones*, 388].

[43] *Iurisc. in l. 1 . in & praeteres ff. de offic. perfest* [Straccha, *Tractatus de mercatura*, in Landry, *De mercatura decisiones*, 388–89].

[44] Straccha, *Tractatus de mercatura*, [in Landry, *De mercatura decisiones*, 387].

[45] Diodorus Siculus, *De rebus antiquis* 2.2 [probably from Zwinger, *Theatrum humanae vitae*, 18.5, 3410].

[46] Aristophanes, *Acharnenses* 738 [LCL 178:147].

[47] Gen. 33:19.

[48] Horace, *Carmina* 1.24 [LCL 33:69].

this world, but to shepherds? "Because God wanted to make himself known above all to these men who engaged in upright commerce, without plundering, defrauding, or suppressing their neighbor."[49] We need to follow in their footsteps so as to please God. Therefore, "let us put off the old man with his deeds,"[50] and that can only happen if "all malice is laid aside, all deceit, hypocrisy, envy, and all disparaging talk."[51] Let us constantly be on watch that "there is not only no cheating or wrongdoing in all who conduct business, but rather that not even the suspicion of fraud or the slightest mark of wrongdoing be found in them."[52] Whoever refuses to be cautious or give attention to this matter cannot escape fraud, crime, or outrage. However, those who do pay careful attention will not venture through fraud "to rob anyone of anything for himself and his own benefit."[53]

15. Three arguments proving the necessity for a merchant to remain honest in his dealings when buying or selling.

[1.] The prudence by which one aspires to the worship of the Christian religion is worthy of praise. But "who among you seems to be religious"?[54] If someone wavers in his honesty, "he deceives his own heart, and his faith is useless."[55] This is because the one cannot be without the other. Therefore, the value you attach to being religious toward God (which you profess) ought to be matched by your concern for good faith and truth, without which religion is to be considered useless, "since it is wrong for him who is eager for the truth to be false

---

[49] Abraham Scultetus, *Idea concionum dominicalium* [(Hannover, 1610), 64].

[50] Col. 3:9.

[51] 1 Peter 2:1.

[52] Cicero, *De officiis* [could not be found].

[53] [Paraphrase of] Cicero, *De officiis* 3.75 [LCL 30:347].

[54] James 1:26.

[55] Ibid.

in any respect and to depart from that very truth which he follows."⁵⁶ In this path of religion we must follow pure honesty. "For [religion] itself must be reverenced, but not its image, and it must be reverenced not by some sacrifice or incense or solemn imprecation, but by the will and a right mind."⁵⁷ "A pure soul is the best possible worship of God."⁵⁸ And as Hermes the Egyptian accurately observed, "The only worship of God is to not be evil."⁵⁹ When this is preserved, religion is preserved in the pious, "through which the life of the soul is sustained, fortified, governed."⁶⁰

2. Next, the good that honesty brings to man demonstrates that "he is bound to work so that he might show himself to be like the God he worships."⁶¹ But how can that be achieved? "By imitating him in desiring to do good to everyone and harm to no one."⁶² He indeed fears and loves God, and will be loved by God. From this it follows that "the (Christian) merchant's home ought to be full of truth and good faith."⁶³

3. What? Should not everyone pursue a good name, and with Phocion ("who on account of what he did was called 'the good' in a

---

⁵⁶ Lactantius, *De vero cultu* [*Divinarum institutionum libri VII*] 6.18 [FC 49:444].

⁵⁷ Lactantius, *De falsa religione* [*Divinarum institutionum libri VII*] 1.20 [FC 49:78].

⁵⁸ [Pseudo-]Seneca, [*Proverbia Senecae* 28, taken from Lipsius, *Politica*, 1.3; Waszink, 269].

⁵⁹ Hermes Trismegistus [taken from Lipsius, *notae* to *Politica*, 3; Waszink, 727].

⁶⁰ Lactantius, *De ira Dei* 12 [FC 54:89].

⁶¹ Arrian, *Epicteti Dissertationes* [probably 2.8.19; LCL 131:257; trans. note: I read *laborare* for *laberare*].

⁶² Seneca, *De quatuor virtutibus*. [This work is currently attributed to Martin of Braga and known as *Formula vitae honestae* 5; FC 62:94.]

⁶³ Étienne Bertrand, [*Consilia* 2.253; taken from Straccha, *De mercatura*, in Landry, *De mercatura decisiones*, 388].

public gathering and by general consent"[64]) see to it that he is called "good" in light of his virtue and honesty? Yes, for "there is no object of such value or any advantage so worth the winning that, to gain it, one should sacrifice the name of a 'good man' and the luster of his reputation. What is there that your so-called 'profit' can bring to you that will compensate for what it can take away, if it steals from you the name of a 'good man' and causes you to lose your sense of honor and justice?"[65] Indeed, it strips away more than Diomedes with his cunning snatched from Glaucus, "who gave gold for bronze."[66] Therefore, let everyone delight in seeking a good name above all other good things, not by the expression he bears or by his dress, but by honesty and truth. "A good man would never rob anyone of anything to enrich himself."[67] "A good man is one who helps everybody he can and harms nobody."[68]

16. Two advantages that accrue to merchants when they conduct their business honestly. First, it aims at and bolsters the marks of one's honor.

In order that merchants might be incited to protect their honesty in all their words and actions, we will explore its advantage. There are two parts to this: the first pertains to the badges of one's own honor, the other to the reputation of the family. For he who is least deceitful can always take pride in all his possessions if he obtained them in a just manner and with good faith. Indeed, with his face uncovered and in the sight of all he can proclaim these words of that holy man: "Here I am. Witness against me before the Lord and before his anointed:

---

[64] Suidas [possibly taken from Zwinger, *Theatrum humanae vitae*, 6.3, 1600].

[65] Cicero, *De officiis* 3.82 [LCL 30:355].

[66] Homer, *Ilias* 6.236 [LCL 170:279].

[67] Cicero, *De officiis* 3.75 [LCL 30:347].

[68] Cicero, *De officiis* 3.76 [LCL 30:347].

Whose ox have I taken, or whose donkey have I taken, or whom have I cheated?"[69] To which they responded, "You have not cheated us."[70]

Can one have a better reputation than that? Does a Christian have anything that brings him greater advantage than to hear people with his own ears recollecting and honoring his kindness and justice? Is there anything that brings greater honor to a free and upright man ("throwing open his home and admitting the whole city to view his possessions"[71]) than to be able to say always and in the presence of all: "If any one recognizes anything as his own, let him take it."[72] "O! a great man, O! a man excellently rich, if after these words he shall possess just as much! I mean this: if without risk and concern he has allowed the people to make search, if no man shall have found in his possession a single thing to lay his hands upon, then he will be rich boldly and in all openness."[73] O! home and household excellently rich, "if no injustice is attached to the acquisition of property."[74] Believe me, nothing makes a person more excellent than to have obtained all his possessions with honesty. "For all things just are proper; all things unjust, like all things immoral, are improper."[75]

17. The second advantage: it increases the reputation of one's family and children.

Let us now move on to the second advantage, which pertains to the reputation of one's family. "Do you set some store by good repute?"[76] That is, do you have the desire to establish a monument of virtue and

---

[69] 1 Sam. 12:3.

[70] 1 Sam. 12:4.

[71] Seneca, *De vita beata* 13 [LCL 254:159].

[72] Ibid.

[73] Seneca, *De vita beata* 13 [LCL 254:159; trans. note: I read *dives* for *duces*].

[74] Solon in Plutarch, *Moralia* (Dinner of the Seven Wise Men) 155D [LCL 222:399].

[75] Cicero, *De officiis* 1.94 [LCL 30.97].

[76] Horace, *Satirae* 2.2 [LCL 194:145].

reputation for your children or posterity? "You should know that you have won enough fame for yourself, enough high rank for your descendants,"[77] if you set greater store by honesty and virtue than by fraud. "For the virtue of ancestors leaves (to one's children) a heritage of renown and dignity,"[78] "and the glory of ancestors is, as it were, a light shining upon their posterity."[79] "Their dowry, and a big one it is, is the virtue they have received from their parents."[80] Indeed (and this is even more delightful), also for children it is the shortest and easiest road to travel, as it were, to fame. "To what did Cicero's son owe the consulship if not to his father? To what did Sextus Pompeius and the other Pompeii, unless it was the greatness of one man?"[81]

What, then, will adorn the offspring of a Christian if not the recollection of virtue and honesty? "[For] the noblest heritage that is handed down from fathers to children, and one more precious than any inherited wealth, is a reputation for virtue and worthy deeds; and to dishonor this must be branded as a sin and a shame."[82] Only then can a father boast before his son "to whom belong the inheritance of his reputation and the duty of imitating his just deeds."[83] So, too, a son can rejoice before his father, whose greatness has made him great. For if anyone "should be eager to ask about details, 'Whose [son is he]? What is his origin? What fellow is this? What was his father?'"[84]—the son who does not lack the better thing and has rather been established by the virtue of his parents may openly respond, "'This is the stock, this is the father from which I boast to have sprung,'[85] who has kept

---

[77] Tacitus, *Historiae* 2.48 [LCL 111:241].

[78] Sallust, *Epistulae ad Caesarem senem de re publica* 2.3 [LCL 522:521].

[79] Sallust, *Bellum jugurthinum* 23 [LCL 116:353].

[80] Horace, *Carmina* 3.24 [LCL 33:199].

[81] Seneca, *De beneficiis* 4.30 [LCL 310:267].

[82] Cicero, *De officiis* 1.121 [LCL 30:125].

[83] Cicero, [*De officiis* 1.78; LCL 30:79].

[84] Horace, *Satirae* 1.6 [LCL 194:79; trans. note: I read *cuius* for *cuias*].

[85] Zwinger, *Theatrum humanae vitae*, 3.[10], 1026 [originally from Diogenes Laertius, *Vitae philosophorum* (Bion) 4.7.47; LCL 184:425].

his hands from the possessions of others, who acted honestly, and who did all other things by which 'he gained a great reputation for himself among his posterity.'[86] And these images of me, as well as my nobility and reputation, make me 'an imitator and emulator of my father's virtue.'"[87]

Come now, O merchants, have you turned your minds to grasp this profit? Indeed, if you apply your mind to it, you will not fail to be moved by the desire for that great thing, winning admiration as not only the scourge of all fraud, but also the defender of all trust. "Onward, (therefore), full of vigor and (good faith), to leave to posterity the fame which you received from your ancestors."[88]

---

[86] Sallust, *Bellum jugurthinum* [actually from Tacitus, *Histories* 2.50; LCL 111:243].

[87] Isocrates, *Orationes* [*Ad Demonicum* 11; LCL 209:11].

[88] Curtius [*Historiae Alexandri Magni* 4.14.25; LCL 368:301].

4

Pursue the Duties of Justice

18. The fourth duty of piety to which the merchant ought to devote himself is the pursuit and love of justice.

If we want to examine the course of commerce further, we will understand also the truth of this statement: "Even (equity) could not remain unaffected, when the size of the fees was the point regarded."[1] "For the nature of each and every person is to love nothing so much as his own interest."[2] But "it is the error of those who are not strictly upright to seize upon something that seems to be expedient and straightaway to dissociate that from the question of moral right."[3] This error is clearly inconsistent with the profession of Christians. Where it is found, "it cancels the honor of a glorious rank by the baseness of unworthy actions."[4] For this reason, in all he does the merchant ought to recall that justice, which is the most excellent virtue, should be cultivated, "preserving right and equity in oneself and in others."[5] "It lays no claim to anyone else's property, and allows everyone to have what is rightfully his; it disregards what is beneficial for self so as to guarantee fairness

---

[1] Tacitus, *Annales* 11.6 [LCL 312:257].

[2] Arrian, *Epicteti dissertationes* 2.22.16 [LCL 131:387].

[3] Cicero, *De officiis* 3.36 [LCL 30:303].

[4] Salvian of Marseille, *De gubernatione Dei*, 3.11 [Sanford, 97].

[5] Lipsius, *Politica*, 2.10 [Waszink, 319].

for all."⁶ Therefore, it "is indispensable for the conduct of business."⁷ "Its importance is so great, that not even those who live by wickedness and crime can get on without some small element of justice. For if a robber takes anything by force or by fraud from another member of the gang, he loses his standing even in a band of robbers; and if the one called the 'Pirate Captain' should not divide the plunder impartially, he would be either murdered or deserted by his comrades. Why, they say that robbers even have a code of laws to observe and obey. And so, because of his impartial division of booty, Bardulis, the Illyrian bandit, of whom we read in Theopompus, acquired a great treasure."⁸

Since justice has such force that it even secures and increases the wealth of brigands, how much do we think its power will contribute to maintaining the wealth deriving from commerce and how great ought we to consider its capacity for sustaining human interaction and society? Therefore, let "buyers and sellers, employers and employees, and all those who are engaged in commercial dealings,"⁹ see to it that they act deliberately and set the duties of justice above all else.

19. Several examples, which show how greatly the duty of justice is to be practiced in all things.

Justice is to be loved. Since it was cherished [even] by the barbarians, it would be most disgraceful if those who have been trained in humanity and piety and initiated in the sacred things of Christ were to depart from it. Some nations pursued[10] justice with so much love that they considered that nothing could be done rightly without it, and therefore

---

[6] Ambrose, *De officiis ministrorum* 1.24.115 [Davidson, 185].

[7] Cicero, *De officiis* 2.40 [LCL 30:209].

[8] Ibid.

[9] Ibid.

[10] [Trans. note: I read *prosequuatae* for *prosequuti*.]

held it up for themselves as "the rule for the greatest uprightness."[11] "All history is full of examples."[12]

The Ethiopians stand out for their devotion to justice. "For their houses have no doors, and although many things are left lying on the street, nothing is stolen."[13] As for the Indians who are called *Padalii*, they in their sacrifices ask the immortal God for little more than justice, "and think that they can be allies to almost all people, if only they pursue justice alone."[14] The Tiberani, an Asian nation neighboring the Chalybians, "are very just."[15] It is reported that the laws pertaining to commerce were given by Bocchoris, the king of the Egyptians, who located all trust in virtue and justice and "assumed that by good morals and righteous acts men would become accustomed to uprightness, lest they seem unworthy of confidence."[16] As for the justice of the Golden Age of humankind, how greatly the poets praised it! "In those days that virgin goddess of great power, Justice, descended with holy honesty from heaven, and ruled the human race mildly on earth."[17]

But if the precepts of justice were not disagreeable to the nations living by nature's guidance, how much more will the Christian submit to them in the desire that "all receive their due."[18] Let no one ever

---

[11] Ambrose, *De officiis ministrorum* [actually from Gregory the Great, *Moralia in Iob* 5.37; MPL 75:717].

[12] Lactantius, *De vero cultu* [*Divinarum institutionum libri VII*] 6.11 [FC 49:408].

[13] Stobaeus, *Sermones* 42 [taken from Zwinger, *Theatrum humanae vitae*, 18.1, 3270, citing Nicolaus Damascenus, *Universali historia seu De moribus gentium libris excepta I. Stobaei collectanea* (s.l., 1593), 15].

[14] Herodotus, book 2 [probably taken from Zwinger, *Theatrum humanae vitae*, 18.1, 3256, which refers to Caelius Rhodiginus, *Lectiones antiquae* 23.19].

[15] *Strabo & Val. Flacc. lib. 5. argum.* [taken from *Dictionarium propriorum nominum virorum, mulierum, populorum, idolorum* (Paris, 1512), 488].

[16] Diodorus Siculus, [*Bibliotheca historica*] 1.79 [LCL 279:271].

[17] [Pseudo-]Seneca, [*Octavia* 397–99; LCL 78:549].

[18] Bernard of Clairvaux, *Sermones* [*de diversis* 19.4 and 125.3; Leclerq 6/1:163, 406].

take anything from anyone, but rather "neglect his own advantages, preferring the common good."[19] For the likeness of that golden time has returned, the Golden Age of the church has returned, and justice has been restored to the earth. "For God, most indulgent parent that he is, when the end of time was drawing near, sent a messenger to bring back that old age and the justice that had been routed, so that the human race would not be thrown about by great and everlasting errors."[20] It therefore remains that all should accept it for themselves and be more motivated by love of their heavenly God and only King to cultivate justice than the ancient men once were, of whom it is reported that they were moved by love for their king (i.e., Saturn) to lead a golden life.[21]

20. The Christian merchant's splendor becomes apparent when he shows himself to be a cultivator of justice.

The splendor of a Christian does not consist in an abundance of commercial undertakings or in the wrongful acquisition of many goods, but rather in the good and just acquisition of the things to which he is entitled. Yet "the virtue of justice is the sovereign mistress and queen of all the virtues."[22] "And it is the foundation of enduring reputation and renown, and without it there can be nothing worthy of praise."[23] For that reason, I prefer to be "stationed as it were on some lofty tower where all might hear."[24] As Virgil said, "Be warned; learn to be just,"[25] so that all might be persuaded by this call and admonition: "No occa-

---

[19] Ambrose, *De paradiso* [3.18; MPL 14:298; FC 42:298].

[20] Lactantius, *De iustitia* [*Divinarum institutionum libri VII*] 5.7 [FC 49:343].

[21] [Next to this section there is a general reference to] Aratus, *Phaenomena*.

[22] Cicero, *De legibus* 1 [actually Cicero, *De officiis* 1:28; LCL 30:295; trans. note: I read *Iustitae* for *Iustitia*].

[23] Cicero, *De officiis* 1.71 [LCL 30:247].

[24] Lactantius, *De origine erroris* [*Divinarum institutionum libri VII*] 2.2 [FC 49:100].

[25] Virgil, *Aeneid* 6.620 [LCL 63:575].

sion arises that can excuse a man for being guilty of injustice."[26] The Spartan king Agesilaus with an epic saying gave elegant expression to the value he attached to justice when, on hearing that the Persian king was called "The Great King," protested: "In what is he greater than I, unless he be more just?"[27] For in his estimation, "No possession is more splendid and honorable for a man, especially a commander, than virtue and justice."[28] "For the dignity of a just man alone will remain among both men and gods."[29] Do you prefer to have an example of this truth? "And behold, there was a man in Jerusalem whose name was Simeon, and this man was just and devout."[30] He is called "just" so that we might be taught by his example. "Those who have passed into the kingdom of light are freed from darkness and their works of darkness, and perform works of light, piety, and integrity."[31] So, too, all those who seek to aspire to that felicity and dignity are bound by that same law of piety and justice. "For thus it is fitting for us to fulfill all righteousness."[32] Therefore, whenever business undertakings are being crafted or pursued, every act and move of the mind must be executed according to the norm of justice from which a pious mind of great constancy should never deviate.

21. One should not only start with the duty of justice but also persevere in it.

I know that the name of justice attracts many, who therefore begin to develop a delight for it, but with a feeble mind. For where the hope of profit begins to fill their mind, "they have no sense of justice or of

---

[26] Cicero, *De officiis* 1.64 [LCL 30:67].

[27] Plutarch, *Moralia* (How a Man May Become Aware of His Progress in Virtue) 78D [LCL 197:419].

[28] Xenophon, *Anabasis* 7.741 [LCL 90:635].

[29] Lang, *Loci communes*, 342v (s.v. *iustitia*) [citing the Greek comedians].

[30] Luke 2:25.

[31] Jodocus Nahumius, [*Conciones in omnia Evangelia* (Hanau, 1609)], *dominica I. post nativ.*, 81.

[32] Matt. 3:15.

what is right and proper."[33] "They follow an honorable course as long as it encourages their expectations, ready to veer across to the opposite course if crooked conduct shall promise more."[34] Consider Glaucus the Spartan, the son of Epicydides, "who was of such distinguished and spotless justice that many came from abroad to Sparta in order to see him, which he later, however, by grave dishonesty and injustice obfuscated to the disgrace of his entire family."[35]

Not so for the person who wants to be strong in true virtue and justice. For such a man "guards the ornaments of all virtues as well as justice"[36] and "fights with implacable hostility against every possible vice."[37] We read that Aristides the Athenian used to be just in every way. For Theophrastus testifies that "he was strictly just in his private relations and toward his fellow citizens."[38] But how would he have distinguished himself by that emblem if he had only exercised justice for a limited time? Is it not because he cultivated justice persistently and without interruption that he acquired a reputation of justice among his fellow men? Let us listen to his testimony. When he was asked by Nicias "how he had become just,"[39] according to the report of Eutropolis, Aristides answered that it was "first of all by the great benefit which nature had bestowed on him, and then also by his own constancy and diligence."[40]

Where these things are absent, no one can obtain a reputation for justice. And so when some praised the people of Elis because they

---

[33] Terence, *Hauton timorumenos* [l. 642; LCL 22:249].

[34] Seneca, *Epistulae morales* 115.10 [LCL 77:327].

[35] Herodotus, [*Historiae*] book 2 [actually the Glaucus episode reported in 6.86; LCL 119:237].

[36] Ambrose, *De officiis ministrorum* 1.193 [Davidson, 231].

[37] Ibid.

[38] Caelius Rhodiginus, [*Lectiones antiquae*] 2.19; and Plutarch, *Aristides* [25; LCL 47:289].

[39] Galen, *De cognoscendis curandisque animi morbis* 7, [in *Galeni operum* (Basel, 1542), 2:174].

[40] Ibid.

were very just in conducting the Olympic Games every five years, Agis said, "What great or marvelous accomplishment is it if they show themselves just on only one day in those five years?"[41] He did not think those who failed to cultivate justice with persistent and attentive care worthy of praise for their justice. Therefore, whoever strives after justice and wants to make it his own must stick to its path without wavering: "You must persevere and develop new strength by continuous application."[42] And whoever has his mind set on it will never attempt to deal unjustly with anyone. Indeed, "he will always think that granting favors to another is preferable to enjoying the favors of others,"[43] and "adopt the principle that the greatest reward for him is to serve the interests of others the best he can."[44] For the concern of the just man is "to make sure that his friend's affairs, too, are put on a safe footing."[45]

22. Three arguments to establish that justice should be preserved diligently and in every transaction.

[1.] What ought to spur the merchant on most powerfully to embrace justice is the very will of our one and only God, which the holy apostle brings to clear expression in these words: "The grace of God that brings salvation has appeared to all men, teaching us that, denying ungodliness and worldly lusts, we should live soberly, justly, and piously in the present age."[46] O, what famous words! To them add also the following: "The love of money is a root of all kinds of evil, for which some have strayed from the faith in their greediness, and pierced themselves through with many sorrows. But you, O man of God, flee these things and pursue righteousness, godliness, faith, love, patience, gentleness."[47]

---

[41] Plutarch, *Moralia* (Sayings of Spartans) 215F [LCL 245:289].

[42] Seneca, *Epistulae morales* [16.1; LCL 75:103].

[43] Diogenes Laertius, *Vitae philosophorum* (Bion) 4.7.49 [LCL 184:427].

[44] Terence, prologue to *Hecyra* [50–51; LCL 23:153].

[45] Terence, *Hauton timuromenos* [689; LCL 22:255].

[46] Titus 2:11–12.

[47] 1 Tim. 6:10–11.

Therefore, "keep this motto always on your lips"[48]—and even more in your heart. For from it the following argument can be deduced: What God wills, the eager mind ought to carry out. ("This is what a great mind looks like to God."[49]) God wills justice. Therefore, the willing and diligent mind ought to act justly and "observe the rule of justice."[50]

2. To this can be added another argument drawn from the very strength and logic of the Christian calling. It orders us "to keep the unity of the Spirit in the bond of peace."[51] It contains within itself "the unity of faith"[52] and teaches us that "we are called in one hope."[53] By that logic it at the same time constrains us to maintain justice in our dealings with others. Indeed, "the bond of blood and goodwill to man binds together by love for one another, so that justice is preserved, and it is important to have memories of the forefathers in that respect."[54] ("For if we have been created by one God, and sprung from one man, and are linked together by the law of blood-kinship, we ought, in consequence, to love all mankind. Not only should we refrain from causing injury, we must not avenge it when done to us, that in us innocence may be perfect."[55]) Yet there is no more excellent society, no firmer bond, than that of Christian calling, that is, to be joined by the bond of one Spirit, faith, and hope. Since Christian merchants say that they have been initiated into these sacred things and claim that they have been clothed in the white robe of religion, they are to cultivate justice among themselves and see to it that "they never take

---

[48] Juvenal, *Satirae* 14 [LCL 91:475].

[49] Seneca, *Epistulae morales* 98 [actually 71.16; LCL 77:83].

[50] Seneca, *De quatuor virtutibus cardinalibus* [currently attributed to Martin of Braga and known as *Formula vitae honestae* 9; FC 62:97].

[51] Eph. 4:3.

[52] Eph. 4:5.

[53] Ibid.

[54] Cicero, *De officiis* 1.55 [LCL 30:59].

[55] Lactantius, *Epitome divinarum institutionum* 65 [Blakeney 113].

up a case in opposition to the right nor in defense of the wrong, and that private citizens are not deprived of their rightful property."56

3. Third, let them be taught by reason itself. Reason removes injustice from every life, since "in judgment it commends [the maxim] 'the fairer is the better,'"57 and in matters of trust it posits this rule: "Between honest parties there ought to be honest dealing."58 How great a bridle that is! For can there be any injustice in "the fairer is the better"? Or, how could malicious or unfair dealings be allowed when "there ought to be honest dealing between honest men"? Therefore, all injustice should be removed from making contracts.

23. The fruits that come to those who cultivate justice. First, that they will not be involved in legal quarrels.

Now we must turn to the fruits of justice. For "the possession of justice is a precious thing,"59 and from this spring flow the following benefits. He who abstains from every form of injustice will readily avoid trials and court cases, "untroubled with the thought that he must rise early on the morrow and pass before Marsyas, who says he cannot stand the face of Novius Junior."60 He will be safe from "ill-disposed or greedy advisers, who, animated by hatred or by avarice, add fuel to their strife and inflame their passions."61 "[For] today there are no men more learned in law who create lawsuits than these people, who buy lawsuits if there is no one to have a lawsuit with,"62 "and no public ware was so frankly on sale as the treachery of advocates."63

---

56 Cicero, *De officiis* 2.71, 73 [LCL 30:247, 249].

57 Cicero, *De officiis* 3.61 [LCL 30:331].

58 Ibid.

59 Greek comedian quoted by Lang, *Loci communes*, 342v (s.v. *iustitia*).

60 Horace, *Satirae* 1.6 [LCL 194:87].

61 Aulus Gellius, *Noctes atticae* 2.12 [LCL 195:159].

62 Plautus, *Poenulus* [586–87; LCL 260:59; modern editions give *coctiores* instead of *doctiores*].

63 Tacitus, *Annales* 11.5 [LCL 312:255].

On the Duties of Merchants

O how blessed is the man who can "take carefree meals,"[64] far removed from legal affairs! He has nothing to fear from the loquacious procurator who has been educated not "toward virtue but 'argued' evil,"[65] who, "to ensnare other people's possessions with a white net,"[66] does not hesitate to take the innocent to court, to harass the guiltless, to assail the unarmed. For "the greedy and hateful money hawk, daring, stealing, thieving as he is,"[67] "holds his hand out even on his deathbed."[68] "What an expert lawyer he is!"[69] How much misfortune is avoided by the man who has no need "to lie prostrate at your cruel doorway, exposed to the North Winds,"[70] seeking counsel. That, indeed, is not what a good and just man fears. "Sweet repose sates him. Set in an obscure place, he enjoys gentle leisure."[71]

24. Other fruits that those who cultivate justice acquire.

There are also other benefits that come to good men from their patronage of justice. Men of old considered "justice the dispenser of good things."[72] But let us consider it the storehouse of every good thing. From it comes the favor which God showers upon men. Yet it is to the just that the God of justice shows his favor. This is why in Euripides, Theseus, when he is pulling out for war against the Thebans with his people, speaks these words: "I need only one thing more, to have as

---

[64] Seneca, *Thyestes* [450–51; LCL 78:271].

[65] Lactantius, *De false religione* [*Divinarum institutionum libri VII*] 1.1 [FC 49:16].

[66] Plautus, *Persae* 73–74 [LCL 163:463].

[67] Plautus, *Persae* 409–10 [LCL 163:503].

[68] Caelius Rhodiginus, [*Lectiones antiquae*] 18:25 [taken from Erasmus, *Adagia*, 7.2.46; CWE 34:24].

[69] Cicero, *Pro Flacco* [84; LCL 324:533].

[70] Horace, *Carmina* 3.10 [LCL 33:173].

[71] Seneca, *Thyestes* [393–95; LCL 78:267].

[72] Zwinger, *Theatrum humanae vitae* [could not be found].

my allies the gods who reverence justice."[73] As such, he made justice's great reward the victory in battle. But we Christians, who do not have fictitious gods but "have rejected the teaching of savage peoples as well as their monstrous and strange rites, and being taught the true religion serve the true God"[74]—how much more abundantly can we imagine God's favor and aid for ourselves, if only we devote ourselves to the cultivation of justice here on earth? A just man pleases God, and "the recollection of the just man is blessed, but the name of the wicked will rot."[75] And "he who performs justice will be exalted."[76] Moreover, the vine of the just also brings forth the most plentiful fruits of many earthly blessings. For "if you look after something soberly or properly, it usually shapes up well under your hands. And as everybody looks after his own business, so is his result afterward; if he is bad or useless, the things he does turn out badly, but if he is decent, they turn out properly."[77] "Blessings are on the head of the righteous, but violence covers the mouth of the wicked."[78]

Moreover, the destiny of the just is a happy end to their life. For while "everything that is sweet beyond the bounds of justice has a very bitter end in store,"[79] on the contrary, "the man who acts equitably will have a beautiful end to his life."[80] After the present life (according to God's gracious benevolence), the just man will also obtain an everlasting reward for his justice. For "he who sows justice will have a sure reward."[81] And just as a curse [*anathema*] awaits the wicked, so a garland [*anadema*] awaits the good. Therefore, "the most excellent

---

[73] Euripides, *Supplices* [594–95; LCL 9:71].

[74] Alexander of Alexandria, [*Geniales dies*] 6.26.

[75] Prov. 10:7.

[76] Sir. 20:30.

[77] Plautus, *Persae* [449–54; LCL 163:507].

[78] Prov. 10:6.

[79] Pindar, [*Isthmians* 7.47–48; taken from Erasmus, *Adagia*, 3.3.52; CWE 34:298].

[80] Lang, *Loci communes*, 342v (s.v. *iustitia*) [citing the Greek comedians].

[81] Prov. 11:18.

profit is not to act unjustly."[82] So let us never spare any effort to keep ourselves and our actions within the limits of justice, so as to pluck its most beautiful fruits.

---

[82] Thucydides, [*Historiae de bello Peloponnesiaco* (Wittenberg, 1580), 49].

5

PURSUE HUMILITY OF MIND

25. The fifth duty of piety required of the merchant is to put off all pride that excessively swells the minds consumed by prosperity.

For the rest, one must note that an easy path to the justice that we have just treated is available, if only the poison of pride—that is, every exaltation of the mind—is destroyed. I define this pride as "an inordinate desire for and delight in human praise."[1] More broadly, I say it is "a wicked movement that despises the humble [and] strives to lord it over superiors and equals."[2] I locate its growth generally in all prosperity: "Prosperity tests the spirit with sharper goads."[3] In particular it is the increase of wealth; for "pride is a common defect in the nobles"[4] and "the paramount danger for men of wealth."[5]

This often happens to merchants. "When they have come into a bit of money, they get above themselves,"[6] and when things happen at will, immediately they are "attended by blind self-love and by glory

---

[1] Alexander de Ales, *Sermones* 2 [could not be found].

[2] Hugo [of St. Victor; could not be found].

[3] Tacitus, *Annales* 1 [actually *Histories* 1.15; LCL 111:31].

[4] Sallust, [*Bellum jugurthinum* 64; LCL 116:311].

[5] Augustine, *in libro supputat.* [actually *Enarrationes in Psalmos* 136.13; WSA 3/20:234].

[6] Terence, *Hecyra* [506; LCL 23:199].

that holds her empty head far too high."[7] They love to walk with head held high, and the only thing that occupies their mind "is the leprosy of pride based in the ownership of their possessions."[8] I do not believe that greater pride and haughtiness was displayed even by Valerius with his curule chair, Padyrius with his myrtle wreath, Aemilius in the victor's purple, Pompeius with his laurel crown, or Julian[9] with his ostentatious diadem "illumined with large gleaming jewels."[10] Why? They say, "Pride suit[s] good fortunes."[11] O how wretched and unmindful of the human condition they are! And those who "measure their own shadow"[12] will hardly find it greater than before. "They may strut around as proudly as they like on account of their money—fortune does not alter breeding."[13] Therefore, we do well to place the vanity and inconstancy of possessions before our eyes and to show that there is no reason to be proud.

26. The rich merchant has no good reason for pride.

Show yourself, you "who want to excel your brother in reproving!"[14] What are the things of which you proudly declare yourself the rightful owner? Does the greatness of your honor give you reason to be proud? You should know that "no man has ever been so far advanced by fortune that she did not threaten him as greatly as she had previously indulged him."[15] "Fortune, reveling in her cruel business, and determined to play her high-handed game, switches her fickle favors, kind now to

---

[7] Horace, *Carmina* 1.18 [LCL 33:61].

[8] Bernard of Clairvaux, *Sermones in die paschae* 3.1 [Leclercq 5:103–4].

[9] Carolus Sigonius, *Historiarum de occidentali imperio* [(Bologna, 1578), 6].

[10] [Pseudo-]Cicero, *Rhetorica ad Herennium* 4.47 [LCL 403:381].

[11] Plautus, *Stichus* [300; LCL 328:47].

[12] Plutarch, *Moralia* (Sayings of Spartans) 218F [LCL 245:309].

[13] Horace, *Carmina* 4.4 [LCL 33:279].

[14] Ambrose, *Sermones* [probably taken from Lang, *Loci communes*, 281r (s.v. *humilitas*), which has *repugnando* instead of *regnando*].

[15] Seneca, *Epistulae morales* 4.7 [LCL 75:17].

me, now to someone else."[16] Think of Alcibiades, "to whom came outstanding nobility of birth, abundant riches, striking good looks, the ready favor of his countrymen, the highest commands, the most ardent intelligence. But what awaited him was judicial condemnation, poverty, his country's hatred, and finally a violent death."[17] And so "the man attended by a favorable fortune was quickly deserted by her, as though she were weary."[18]

What then if the honors you receive make you like Herod? "They are bestowed not by virtue, but by circumstance."[19] They come to you suddenly, only to dissolve unexpectedly again. They are not firmly rooted in any place or person. Consider how disdainfully Herod acted when he was at the apex of his dignity and ruling. He may have appeared to the crowd "arrayed in royal apparel,"[20] but was he not reduced to weakness when "the unexpected death blow carried him off"?[21] "Then immediately an angel of the Lord struck him, because he did not give glory to God. And he was eaten by worms and died."[22] See how nothing is so firm that there is no threat of losing it.

But perhaps you will continue and show me your piles of wealth. Why? Are you, like Hezekiah, proud because of your wealth? O wretched and vain man! "All human affairs are uncertain, and the higher you climb the more slippery your position."[23] "Frail and fragile surely and like children's toys are the so-called power and wealth of humankind."[24] No mortal thing is of lasting duration. While you

---

[16] Horace, *Carmina* 3.4 [LCL 33:215].

[17] Valerius Maximus, [*Factorum ac dictorum memorabilium*] 6.11 [LCL 493:97].

[18] Gaius Vellius Paterculus, [*Historiae*] 2.69.6 [LCL 152:201].

[19] Cicero, *De domo sua* [58; LCL 158:309].

[20] Acts 12:21.

[21] Horace, *Carmina* 2.13 [LCL 33:123].

[22] Acts 12:23.

[23] Tacitus, *Annales* [1.72; LCL 249:367].

[24] Valerius Maximus, [*Factorum ac dictorum memorabilium*] 6.9.ext.7 [LCL 493:99].

hold the happiness of the world, you are losing it. Riches are earthly goods. "All this, won by long and arduous toil, a single hour snatched from him."[25] I believe that, by reading the Holy Scriptures, you have sufficiently understood how fleeting King Hezekiah's riches really were, plundered by the Babylonians. Why, then, do you think yours will remain forever? Why do you boast in what is yours?—"as though anything were one's own, which in a moment of flitting time, now by prayer, now by purchase, now by force, now by final destiny, changes owners and passes under the power of another. Thus since to none is granted lasting use, and heir follows another's heir as wave follows wave, what advantage are estate and wealth or granaries?"[26]

27. The same argument as the previous section: a reason for pride is taken away from the merchant.

I believe that the possession of many acres makes your minds proud. For what do I sometimes hear people say? "I have many goods laid up for many years."[27] Or, I feel like "Dorylas, the richest man in the land of Nasamonia—Dorylas, rich in land, whom none surpassed in domain or piles of spices."[28] Do these things raise your minds even higher? What a fool you are, who dares to take pride in his many fields. Show me your fields and estates on a map and you will see "that they are not marked anywhere."[29] "Are you then proud of properties that are not a fraction of the earth?"[30] Remember also that the whole circle of our earth "is but a point in comparison with the extent of the whole heavens."[31] Could you have abundance on that point? And yet you boast in the wide possession of fields? No, you will say, I am wild at heart, I thoroughly enjoy the pleasures of the world. But, I beg

---

[25] Cicero, *Pro Sulla* [73; LCL 324:387].

[26] Horace, *Epistulae* 2.2 [LCL 194:439].

[27] Luke 12:19.

[28] Ovid, *Metamorphoses* 5 [LCL 42:247].

[29] Claudius Aelianus, [*Varia historia*] 3:28 [LCL 486:163].

[30] Ibid.

[31] Boethius, [*De consolatione philosophiae*] 2.7 [LCL 74:217].

you, consider how you boast in something filled with misery and in a happiness devoid of true blessedness. "Vicious and death-bringing pleasures do not make a person happy, nor does opulence, the enkindler of lusts, by which a human soul, ensnared and shackled to the body, is doomed to eternal death."[32] Yet "if anyone loves the world, the love of the Father is not in him. And the world is passing away, and the lust of it."[33] Therefore, how filthy you are when you so love the world that it kindles you to arrogance and drives you to ruin. But now you see (I think) that neither you nor even the most successful man has any reason to boast. Show yourself different, therefore. "You will be wise to shorten your sail when it swells before too favorable a breeze."[34]

28. God utterly hates pride.

Plautus is right when he says, "He who looks too high seems to meet evil."[35] To these words I would add: he who looks too high does not just seem, but really does meet evil. "A proud mind never has firm ground to stand on; the great peaks of vast empires fall because it is forgotten that men are feeble."[36] "Do you not know that it is when you have climbed from a deep well up to the top that you are in the greatest danger of falling back down again?"[37] But the proud "do their business at the top of the well and therefore fall in."[38] For "every proud person is an abomination to the Lord."[39] "Many are excessively distinguished and renowned, but the secrets are revealed to the gentle. For the power of God is great, but it is from the humble that he takes his glory."[40]

---

[32] Lactantius, *De ira Dei* [24; FC 54:115].

[33] 1 John 2:15, [17].

[34] Horace, *Carmina* 2.10 [LCL 33:117].

[35] [Pseudo-]Plautus, in *Pseudolus* 22.

[36] Seneca the Elder, *Suasoriae* 2.3 [LCL 464:511–13].

[37] Plautus, *Miles gloriosus* [1150–51; LCL 163:267].

[38] Plautus, *Miles gloriosus* [1152; LCL 163:267].

[39] Prov. 16:[5].

[40] Sir. 3:20 [Vulgate].

"The Lord God has sworn by himself, the Lord God of hosts says: 'I abhor pride.'"[41] For just as a lightning bolt destroys the hard things that stand unyielding in its way but does no harm to things that are pliant and readily give way, so too God "resists the proud, but gives grace to the humble."[42] "There is one that humbles and that exalts."[43] He wants nothing exalted above himself. "An avenging God follows at the back of the proud."[44] It is his "to humble the proud and to exalt the humble."[45] Therefore, "put off your haughtiness, which is displeasing to God, otherwise the rope may run back as the wheel spins."[46]

29. Two examples to illustrate the gravest and most certain punishment awaiting the proud.

Most wretched indeed is anyone incited by a fury of heedless ambition thirsting for extravagant glory and enflamed with an incessant and unparalleled desire for power. For "those who strive to reach the top will fall with the very branches they have grasped."[47] Reflect on the old, consider the new: "The more your reflect on events recent or remote, the more you are haunted by the sense of a mockery in human affairs."[48] "I will quote just a few instances from all those that the past supplies, and then say no more on this point."[49] The first person to occur to me was the proud Haman,[50] who "began to be crazed by the prosperity which surrounded him, forgetting the condition from which the

---

[41] Amos 6:8.

[42] James 4:6.

[43] Sir. 7:12.

[44] Seneca, *Hercules* [385; LCL 62:45].

[45] Diogenes Laertius, *Vitae philosophorum* (Chilon) [1.3.69; LCL 184:71].

[46] Horace, *Carmina* 3.10 [LCL 33:173].

[47] Curtius, [*Historiae Alexandri Magni*] 7.8.14 [LCL 369:201].

[48] Tacitus, *Annales* 3.18 [LCL 249:551].

[49] Cicero, *Pro Cluentio* [133; LCL 198:363–65].

[50] Est. 7.

kindness of his king had saved him."[51] For although King Artaxerxes had elevated him to great riches and power, "there arose, of course, those vices which tend to be fostered by prosperity: promiscuity and pride."[52] But what punishment followed? See the executioner standing behind him who, on the following day, before "the light was gone and the sun was making ready to take the yokes from his shining steeds,"[53] exchanged pride for the greatest pain and disgrace. For "Haman was hanged on the gallows that he had prepared for Mordecai."[54] What a change that was! "Such joy, and now such sorrow!"[55] Nor can things be any different for the proud. "[For] when pride comes, there is shame,"[56] and "the Lord destroys the house of the proud."[57]

For another example of punished pride, consider King Nebuchadnezzar. He who, "flushed by success, lapsed into arrogance,"[58] was punished by "being changed into a beast."[59] This change, as Epiphanius says, "was in his perception and in that of those who saw him, rather than the form or substance of nature."[60] However it may be, his and the previous punishment should constantly be held up before your eyes as worthy examples. Learn here how he "who shrinks back from works of humility falls from the dignity of his office by the weight of his pride."[61] See here how "God overturns the thrones of proud

---

[51] Curtius, *Historiae Alexandri Magni* 10.2.22 [LCL 369:489].

[52] Sallust, *Bellum jugurthinum* [41; LCL 116:261].

[53] Ovid, [*Heroides* 21, lines 85–86; [LCL 41:299].

[54] Est. 7:10.

[55] Pliny the Younger, *Epistulae* 5.16 [LCL 55:381].

[56] Prov. 11:2.

[57] Prov. 15:25.

[58] Tacitus, *Annales* 11.17 [LCL 312:275].

[59] Dan. 4:[33].

[60] Epiphanius [as cited in, for example, Johannis Aquilanus, *Sermones Quadragesimales* (Venice, 1576), 142].

[61] John Chrysostom, *Policratico libro* 4 [probably taken from Lang, *Loci communes*, 281v (s.v. *humilitas*)].

princes."[62] Think here of the critical state of the ungodly, how "great trees are long in growing, but are uprooted in a single hour."[63] So it is with the proud. Great today? Nobody tomorrow. Therefore, "may the other's failings strike you with shame,"[64] since (and I am not a messenger of useless things to you) "there is punishment in store for you, unless you cease to be proud."[65]

30. *A humble mind recommended to the merchant.*

Since it is through pride that the greatest things become the basest and that people are dispelled from their highest ranks, we do well to seek all lofty things in the kingdom of humility, while it is "'modesty,' which is called ταπεινοφροσύνη, from φρονήματος, that is, 'spirit,' and from ταπείνωσις, that is, 'humiliation.'"[66] Everyone ought to embrace it as if it were "a medicine making provision for all, deflating what is distended, renewing what is wasting away, cutting away what is superfluous, curing what is corrupted."[67] "Humility is a glorious thing,"[68] since it is the source of virtue, and "while pride usually grows from all good taken, humility alone is the rampart and tower of all virtues."[69] It makes us acceptable to God and people, since a forthright and upright mind pleases him, and "there is nothing that renders us so acceptable to both people and God as to be low with humility rather than high

---

[62] Sir. 10:17 (Vulgate).

[63] Curtius, [*Historiae Alexandri Magni*] 7.8.14 [LCL 369:201].

[64] Horace, *Epistulae* 1.18 [LCL 194:375].

[65] Albius Tibullus, [*Carmina* 77; LCL 6:237].

[66] Augustine, *Epistulae* 18 [probably taken from Lang, *Loci communes*, 281r (s.v. *humilitas*), who refers to Anton. & Maxim, *Serm. De humilitate*; trans. note: I read *dicitur* for *diciter* and *et* for *est*].

[67] Augustine, *Epistulae* 58, [no doubt taken from Lang, *Loci communes*, 281r (s.v. *humilitas*); the quotation is actually from Augustine, *De agone christiano* 11.12; FC 2:330].

[68] Bernard of Clairvaux, *Liber de gradibus humilitatis et superbiae* [47; Leclercq 3:56; Evans 136].

[69] Bernard of Clairvaux, *Epistulae* [42.17; Leclercq 7:114].

by the merit of the life we live."⁷⁰ "The baser people become in God's sight, the more precious in their own; the more precious before God, the baser for his sake to themselves."⁷¹ Likewise, against the urging of the devil, "it helps us so that we might be victorious, it sets us firm so that we might not desert, and it shows us the way so that we might escape."⁷² Of Anthony the Abbot it is reported that the Spirit took him to see the whole world filled with snares on every side. And when he in astonishment asked, "Who can escape those snares?,"⁷³ the answer he received was "humility."⁷⁴ Since humility can win a great victory for us, we ought to fix our mind on its root, so that there might sprout in us the virtue whose benefit allows us to escape the deceitful snares of our sworn enemy.

31. The diligence with which the saints cultivated the humility that a Christian has to pursue as well.

Indeed, "nothing is more excellent than humility."⁷⁵ Is King David not greater than others in this, that he was incapable of exaltation? "He constructed a great (I assure you) skyscraper of a building on the foundation of humility."⁷⁶ He said, "My heart is not haughty, nor my eyes lofty. Neither do I concern myself with great matters, nor

---

⁷⁰ [Pseudo-]Jerome, *Epistulae* 148 (to Celantia) [probably taken from Lang, *Loci communes*, 281v (s.v. *humilitas*)].

⁷¹ Gregory, *Moralia in Iob* 18.38.59 [Kerns 4:101–2; taken from Lang, *Loci communes*, 281v (s.v. *humilitas*)].

⁷² Zwinger, *Theatrum humanae vitae* [could not be found; instead it might be taken from Lang, *Loci communes*, 165v (s.v. *diabolus*), where it is ascribed to Bernhardus, *In serm.*].

⁷³ Marcus Marulu Spalatensis, [*De religiose vivendi institutione*] 1.5, [in *Opera omnia*, (Antwerp, 1601), 33].

⁷⁴ Ibid.

⁷⁵ Ambrose, *Expositio Evangelii secundum Lucam* 6 [MPL 15:1777].

⁷⁶ Augustine, *De verbis Domini* [*Sermones ad populum* 69.2; WSA 3/3:235; taken from Lang, *Loci communes*, 281r (s.v. *humilitas*)].

with things too profound for me."[77] See how this great man did not consider himself great and took care to keep his mind from the evil of pride. "Have I not," he says, "calmed and quieted my soul, like a weaned child with his mother; like a weaned child is my soul within me?"[78] Following the example of this holy king, the saints pursued such humility of mind—as if it numbered among the other ornaments of the Christian religion—like a precious treasure. As Augustine says, "Redeemer, drive out the spirit of pride from me, and give me the treasure of your humility."[79] Although the sacred doctor requests many other virtues from God in that passage, this is the only one he calls the "treasure of humility," since "it is the one that enriches the mind and disposes it to the other virtues and to the treasure of God's gifts."[80]

Let the Christian therefore humbly request this treasure for himself: "Let him follow humility—not a humility that is put on show or faked by gestures of the body or a broken voice, but the humility that is expressed from the pure state of the heart."[81] "Better to be of a humble spirit with the lowly, than to divide the spoil with the proud."[82] To seek to be elevated above all people is reprehensible; praiseworthy is rather to surpass others in modesty and submission of mind. "Blessed is the person whose life is exalted, but whose mind is humble."[83] Therefore, O merchant, if you want to be considered wise and great in great things, "learn how to bear your fortune well."[84] Do not swell over your riches,

---

[77] Ps. 131:[1].

[78] Ibid.

[79] [Pseudo-]Augustine, *Meditationes* 1 [MPL 40:901; possibly taken from Philippus Diez, *Summa praedicantium, ex omnibus locis communibus locupletissima* (Venice, 1601), 1:459 (s.v. *humilitas*)].

[80] Diez, *Loci communes*, 1:459 (s.v. *humilitas*).

[81] [Pseudo-]Jerome, *Epistulae* 148 (to Celantia) [probably taken from Lang, *Loci communes*, 281v (s.v. *humilitas*)].

[82] Prov. 16:[19].

[83] Cleonicus [no doubt taken from Lang, *Loci communes*, 282r (s.v. *humilitas*), where it is ascribed to Clemens] in Antonius & Maximus.

[84] Horace, *Carmina* 3.27 [LCL 33:209].

but fear for "change in your character, rather than your prosperity."[85] Therefore, "may all you do be seasoned with humility."[86]

32. Some incentives for pursuing humility written down. First, the inconstancy of human affairs.

The fact of the matter is that "pride is mostly born from abundance and the affluence of everything."[87] I say, however, that it deserves great mockery. For what are all the things that accrue to us in this life except inconstancies subject to motion? "Fortune never stands long on the same spot."[88] "The changes in fortune and time are trifling and feeble."[89] Can anyone therefore be called high and excellent by his great mind who proudly applauds himself when the things he acquired quickly leave him? "Due to the inconstancy of things, no one should be haughty or raise their mind in pride over their prosperity."[90]

The noble Romans of antiquity taught that it was a custom that those surpassing the others in wealth and nobility had "to wear little moons on their shoes,"[91] which explains Martial's "crescent shoebuckle"[92] and the satirist's "he sews the crescent to his black shoe."[93] The silent meaning attached to this custom was for them, ever mindful of the inconstancy of things that afflicts the human condition, to be taught to seek what is most humble. Indeed, "the moon regulates the phases

---

[85] Sallust, *Oratio Cottae ad populum Romanum*, [in *Histories* 2; LCL 522:153].

[86] Augustine, *Epistulae* 58 [no doubt from Lang, *Loci communes*, 281r (s.v. *humilitas*); the original source of this quotation could not be found].

[87] Cicero, *De lege agraria* [2.35; LCL 240:473].

[88] Curtius, [*Historiae Alexandri Magni* 4.5.2; LCL 368:207].

[89] Cicero, *De finibus* 5.71 [LCL 40:473].

[90] Zwinger, *Theatrum humanae vitae* 7.2, 1686.

[91] Caelius Rhodiginus, *Lectiones antiquae* 20.28.

[92] [Martial, *Epigrammaton libri* 1.49; LCL 94:77.]

[93] [Juvenal, *Satirae* 7; LCL 91:315, where the editor's note indicates that "the crescent-shaped ivory sewn to the shoe was a sign of patrician or senatorial status."]

of its light under a fixed law of seven-day periods,"[94] "nor can Diana, goddess of the night, have the same phase always."[95] This is the condition of a man who comes forth out of the dark and then shining with a splendid luster soon arises with his face about to be besmeared. But stop! Since he prefers the most brilliant appearance of radiance, he (like the moon) again fades and disappears, until by some reversing logic he again returns to nothing. For that reason, we applaud the view of Totila, the king of the Goths, who turned to his men after taking Rome and said, "Let us not be proud, but rather fix our eyes on God and wait in dread for our fortune to change."[96] This wise king foresaw that human affairs depend on the changing times, that "the vicissitudes of life are short and inconstant, and fortune never shows indulgence without reserve,"[97] and so that "continence and self-control in every exalted fortune are to be considered as eminent good things."[98] This is why the changing and inconstant condition of human affairs should serve as a warning to Christians and urge them to show modesty in the riches they possess. Why? Do "all things that puff us up not come from the outside?"[99] Remember that these things are more changeable than Euripus Strait[100] and will soon pass away like bubbles.

33. The second incentive by which the virtue of humility is instilled is the fragility of human life.

Next, consider what you are: "You ought to estimate your own worth."[101]

---

[94] Macrobius, [*Commentarii in somnium Scipionis* 1.6.54; Stahl 111; possibly taken from Ambrosius Calepino, *Dictionarium* (s.l., 1553), 335r].

[95] Ovid, *Metamorphoses* 15 [LCL 43:379].

[96] Albert Krantz, *Sueciae* [probably *Chronica regnorum aquilonarium Daniae, Sueciae, et Noruagiae* (Frankfurt, 1575), 288].

[97] Curtius, [*Historiae Alexandri Magni*] 4.14.19 [LCL 368:297].

[98] Curtius, [*Historiae Alexandri Magni*] 6.6.1 [LCL 369:49].

[99] Lipsius, [*notae* to *Politica*, 15; Waszink, 745].

[100] [The strait between mainland Greece and the island of Euboa is known for its strong and quickly changing tidal currents.]

[101] Lipsius, *notae* to *Politica*, [15; Waszink, 745].

You are a man from the soil, dust from dust, earth from the earth, and you will dissolve into earth. For "that which once came from earth, to earth returns back again."[102] "How can dust and ashes be proud?"[103] "The king of today will die tomorrow."[104] Philip of Macedonia drew much benefit from the recollection of his great fragility. To avoid being overcome by felicity, this most felicitous king charged one of his children to enter his bedroom every morning at dawn and shout three times: "Philip, remember that you are human!"[105] Why? Because he knew how "success serves as a wonderful screen for vices"[106] and that "human frailty is too often forgotten amid prosperity."[107] Therefore, by the frequent mention of his mortality, "he wanted to put curbs upon his good fortune so as to manage it the more easily."[108] And this is how someone can be moved to put off his pride. For "a bee, meeting treacherous currents of air, will often balance itself in empty space by lifting tiny pebbles, so that the fragile beating of its wings is not driven down by gusts of wind."[109] So, too, anyone who fears that he will be taken in the wrong direction by the wind of empty glory should balance the inclinations of his mind by considering his fleeting state and the passing nature of all things, so that this will humble him as much as his false self-estimation grows, and the sense of his own fragility may persuade him to seek the depths of humility as deeply as the heights to which his arrogance ascends.

---

[102] Lucretius, [*De rerum natura* 2; LCL 181:173].

[103] Sir. 10:9.

[104] Sir. 10:10.

[105] Claudius Aelianus, *Varia historia* 8; Caelius Rhodiginus, *Lectiones antiquae* 10.33.

[106] Sallust, *Oratio Lepidi ad populum Romanum*, [in *Histories* 1; LCL 522:49].

[107] Curtius, [*Historiae Alexandri Magni*] 4.14.20 [LCL 368:297–299].

[108] Curtius, [*Historiae Alexandri Magni*] 7.8.25 [LCL 369:205].

[109] Ambrose, *De virginitate* 1.17.106 [MPL 16:293].

34. The third incentive for seeking humility is the loss of riches on earth after death.

Next, in order to resist your ambition and promote humility, "do not set great store by anything of you except what is yours."[110] Are you persuaded that what you only have as "a traveler has an inn" is really yours?[111] "Anything of which you are entitled the owner is in your possession but is not your own; for there is no strength in that which is weak, nor anything lasting in that which is frail."[112] "You will leave the woodland pastures that you have bought up, and your town house, and your villa; yes, you will leave them, and your heir will take possession of the wealth you have built so high."[113] Reflecting on this near death, the Egyptian sultan Saladin, once the great fear of Christians, admonished his men—late but still earnestly—to hang a linen undergarment on a spear and hold it before his body after death, with a herald crying out, "There is nothing more from all his riches that Saladin, the conqueror of Asia, is taking with him."[114] No doubt this dying man now saw how vain and short-lived the riches were that used to be his pride and during his lifetime had served him as a sign of splendor and the greatest reason for bragging. You, O Christian, who is nowhere close to possessing such a reign—will you then gape at, brag about, and swell up in the idle goods of a mortal? Indeed, "most worthless of all is anyone who convinces himself that the most trifling things are the greatest";[115] "when he dies he shall carry away none of these things; his glory shall not descend after him, nor shall his riches."[116]

---

[110] Lipsius, *notae* to *Politica*, [15; Waszink, 745].

[111] Seneca, *Ad Marciam de consolatione* [actually from Epictetus, *Encheiridion* 11; LCL 218:491].

[112] Seneca, *Epistulae morales* 98.10 [LCL 77:125].

[113] Horace, *Carmina* 2.3 [LCL 33:103].

[114] Jan Dubravius, 14 [*Historiae regni Boiemiae* (s.l., 1552), 86v]; Baptista Fulgosius, 7.2 [*Factorum dictorumque memorabilium* (Paris, 1584), 248; the story about Saladin can be read in Lipsius's *notae*].

[115] John Chrysostom, *Homiliae in epistulam ii ad Corinthios* 1.

[116] Ps. 49:17.

"Earth must be left behind, and home, and beloved wife; and of all the trees that you cultivate none except the abhorrent cypress will follow you, their short-lived master."[117] Free your mind, therefore, from the foolish suggestions of pride, but recognizing the fleeting nature and vanity of the world's possessions keep yourself always at the greatest distance from empty praise and ambition. "Whoever exalts himself will be humbled, and he who humbles himself will be exalted."[118]

---

[117] Horace, *Carmina* 2.14 [LCL 33:125].
[118] Matt. 23:12.

6

SHOW KINDNESS TO THE POOR

35. The sixth duty of piety is to use one's justly acquired wealth to show beneficence to the poor.

Since the apostle thought that the rich of the present age need to be warned "not to be haughty, nor to trust in uncertain riches, but to be rich in good works, ready to give, willing to share,"[1] we do well to set the sixth duty of piety, which concerns beneficence and liberality to the needy, before the merchants of the present age. Indeed, "there is nothing more honorable and noble than to be indifferent to money, if one does not possess it, and to devote it to beneficence and liberality, if one does possess it."[2] I see people straying from that liberality and beneficence in two ways, either by giving nothing or by giving badly. Nothing is given by those among whom "there are so few instances of generosity, and greed for ownership has taken such a hold of them that they seem to be possessed by wealth rather than to possess it."[3] Something is given badly since "nowadays wealth is given only to the rich."[4] "The first rule of duty requires us to lend assistance preferably to people in proportion to their individual need. Most people adopt the contrary course: they put themselves most eagerly at the service

---

[1] 1 Tim. 6:17–18.

[2] Cicero, *De officiis* 1.68 [LCL 30:71].

[3] Pliny the Younger, *Epistulae* 9.30 [LCL 59:143].

[4] Martial, [83; LCL 94:393].

of the one from self-interest, whom they hope to receive the greatest favors, even though he has no need of their help."[5] No value should be attached to such liberality, since "wanting to help the strong is the work of pride."[6] It is a liberality done for reward. For "such persons do not seem to me to part with anything of their own, but use their gifts as baits to hook other people's possessions. Other smart characters rob one person to give to another, hoping their greed will bring them a reputation for generous giving."[7] "The one certain and true office of liberality is to care for the needy and the useless."[8] This is why "I should like to see the truly generous man giving to his country, neighbors, relatives, and friends, but by them I mean his friends without means; unlike the people who mostly bestow their gifts on those best able to make a return."[9] For "to help the weakling is the work of love."[10] In what follows, we will see how much a Christian is committed to the affection of piety.

36. Beneficence to the poor is commanded by God.

It is in no way good that the exercise of beneficence is neglected, since "God wants each person to feel the distress of others as if it were his own, and for God's sake to rush to their aid, just like he himself would want to be aided if he experienced such tribulation."[11] For God did not give wisdom to the rest of the animals, but rather natural defenses to keep them safe from attack. Man, however, he furnished with wisdom,

---

[5] Cicero, *De officiis* 1.49 [LCL 30:53].

[6] Gregory, *Moralia in Iob* 17.18.26 [Kerns 4:28; probably taken from Lang, *Loci communes*, 82r (s.v. *auxilium*)].

[7] Pliny the Younger, *Epistulae* [9.30; LCL 59:143].

[8] Lactantius, *De vero cultu* [*Divinarum institutionum libri VII*] 6.11 [FC 49:424].

[9] Pliny the Younger, *Epistulae* 9.30 [LCL 59:143].

[10] Gregory, *Moralia in Iob* 17.18.26 [Kerns 4:28; probably taken from Lang, *Loci communes*, 82r (s.v. *auxilium*)].

[11] Jerome, *Epistulae* [no doubt taken from Lang, *Loci communes*, 82r (s.v. *auxilium*); the original source for this quotation could not be found].

and "he gave him, besides the others, this affection of piety, in order that man might kindly regard his fellow man and love him and cherish him and furnish him help."[12] And lest man allow this affection of piety to be lost when he forgets his humanity, God also gave him precepts commanding him not "to divert his eyes from the needy,"[13] "to shut his ears to the cry of the poor,"[14] or "to turn his face from the destitute."[15] That is to say, people misuse their mouth or tongue by uttering such horrid words as "Go, and come back, for tomorrow I will give."[16] And God commanded them not to keep their hand from giving aid to "those to whom it is due, when it is in the power of their hand to do so."[17] "He indeed detests closefisted hands,"[18] but he cherishes, adorns, and loves full hands, which give help to others with a pious and pure compassion. Therefore, "he who has mercy on the poor, blessed is he."[19] "Do not reject a suppliant in distress."[20] "Do good to the needy before you die, and reach out and give to the poor as much as you can."[21]

---

[12] Lactantius, *De cultu vero* [*Divinarum institutionum libri VII*] 6.10 [FC 54:417].

[13] Sir. 4:1.

[14] Prov. 21:13.

[15] Sir. 4:[4].

[16] Prov. 3:28.

[17] Prov. 3:27.

[18] Horace, *Carmina* 3.19 [LCL 33:191].

[19] Prov. 14:21.

[20] Sir. [4:4].

[21] Sir. 14:[13].

37. The duty of beneficence proved both by the communion we have as members of Christ's body and by our joining together as living stones of the sacred temple.

Let us be certain that "we are the parts of one great body,"[22] that is, "Christ."[23] For that reason, we ought to take pains "so that this whole body, joined and knit together by what every joint supplies, according to the effective working by which every part does its share, causes growth of the body for the edifying of itself through love."[24] This happens purposely when the strong meet the weak in every way, and "where we strive to be good and kind as much as we can. If we have wealth, if we have resources at hand, let them be used, not for the pleasure of one, but for the welfare of many."[25] Do the members [of the body] not help each other in every way? So too we must help each other "with money or help or good advice."[26] Let us also keep in mind that we have been built up "by Christ, the living stone, so that we might grow"[27] "into a holy temple for God."[28] For "our relations with one another are like a stone arch, which would collapse if the stones did not mutually support each other, and which is upheld in this very way."[29] In fact, our relations are actually like a living arch, since we are "living stones."[30] Why then should this beneficence not be found also in us? Whoever enjoys this corporeal life seeks to show in what he does what kind of mind is living in him. But since this kind of life is more noble—"give

---

[22] Seneca, *Epistulae morales* 95.52 [LCL 77:91].

[23] Eph. 4:12.

[24] Eph. 4:16.

[25] Lactantius, *De ira Dei* 24 [FC 54:115–16].

[26] Plautus, *Pseudolus* [19; LCL 260:245].

[27] 1 Peter 2:4–5.

[28] Eph. 2:22.

[29] [Pseudo-]Seneca, *De moribus* [actually in *Epistulae* 95.53; LCL 77:91].

[30] 2 Peter 2:5.

to the blind, the weak, the lame, the destitute"[31]—shall we hesitate to use our wealth for relieving the poverty of others to show that we truly are alive? Let us give, let us give gifts from our coffers and from our heart; let us pour out libations with hand and mind. As for you, O merchants, "as the elect of God, holy and beloved, put on tender mercies, kindness, supporting one another."[32]

38. Beneficence brings great wages and profit.

It is the soul's wisdom to "sow favor in order to reap fruit."[33] But is anything sweeter than the fruit obtained from showing beneficence? Consider that "whenever someone can show kindness to his neighbor but fails to do so, he should be considered to fall far short of the love of God."[34] Indeed, "to show kindness to a man is to show great service before God."[35] Why was that gentile Cornelius, centurion of an Italian cohort, so thankful to God? Because "he was considered worthy for having spoken with an angel, for having been baptized by an apostle, and for clearly being illuminated by the Holy Spirit."[36] Indeed, his "alms were remembered in the sight of God."[37] What splendid things he acquired by his frailties! Do you want more? He who gives to the poor imitates God. For "a man never resembles God more than when he shows kindness—even though God shows kindness in great things and

---

[31] Lactantius, *De vero cultu* [*Divinarum institutionum libri VII*] 6.11 [FC 49:423].

[32] Col. 3:12–13.

[33] [Pseudo-]Cicero, *Ad populum et equites Romanos antequam erit in exilium* [(Lübeck, 1589), 10r].

[34] Irenaeus, "Letter to Pope Victor," [in Eusebius, *Historia ecclesiastica* 5.24.11–18].

[35] John Chrysostom, *Homil.* 27 [*In Geneseos libros enarrationes* (Antwerp, 1547), 164r; taken from Lang, *Loci communes*, 91v (s.v. *beneficentia*)].

[36] Marulus, *De institutione bene vivendi* 1.2 [probably cited via Herold, *Exempla virtutum et vitiorum*, 1183].

[37] Acts 10:31.

man in what is small, each according to his abilities."[38] Consider also that "whoever shows kindness on earth stores up treasure for himself in heaven."[39] Therefore, "why do you fear to make a passing and fragile good everlasting, or to entrust your treasures to the guardianship of God, where you may fear no thief and robber? He who is rich with God can never be poor."[40] "If farmers empty out their storehouse and commit their seeds to the field, and do so gladly in the hope of reaping greater things, how much more ought we to distribute the things that we have hoarded up uselessly for ourselves for the use of our poor brothers."[41] For "great is the reward of mercy"[42] that the Lord God holds forth out of grace. Therefore, "transfer to a great sacrifice the things which are to badly perish, so that for these real gifts you may have an eternal reward from God."[43] "Let us not grow weary while doing good, for in due season we shall reap if we do not lose heart. Therefore, as we have opportunity, let us do good to all, especially to those who are of the household of faith."[44]

39. The law of nature binds everyone to do good to and help those in need.

Far be it from us to hold the needy in disdain and contempt, such that "nothing may seem more natural than to help those who share in our predicament."[45] For nature dictates that we are people, and that we

---

[38] Gregory of Nazianzus [probably *Orationes* 45; MPG 36:621–62].

[39] John Chrysostom, *Homil.* 55 [could not be found].

[40] Lactantius, *De vero cultu* [*Divinarum institutionum libri VII*] 6.12 [FC 49:430].

[41] John Chrysostom, *Homiliae in Genesim* 55 [taken from Diez, *Loci communes*, 1:313 (s.v. *eleemosyna*)].

[42] Lactantius, *De vero cultu* [*Divinarum institutionum libri VII* 6.12; FC 49:430].

[43] Ibid.

[44] Gal. 6:9–10.

[45] Ambrose, *De officiis ministrorum* [actually *Expositio Evangelii secundum Lucam* 7.84; MPL 15:1720].

are therefore all bound by this law, "that we protect the weakness of nature by mutual assistance, and run to help the one who needs it."[46] To do good to a man is a matter of nature. "Anyone who does not do this robs himself of the name of man, since it is the duty of humaneness to come to the aid of man in necessity and danger."[47] Nature also teaches us that we are all made from the same lump and substance, so that every man is the same thing we are, that is, flesh.[48] "Nature produced us related to one another, since it created us from the same source and to the same end."[49] This implies a great compulsion to help him. For "has anyone ever hated his own flesh?"[50] Does he not rather "nourish and cherish it"?[51] Therefore, it is according to the constitution of nature "more wretched to commit than to suffer injury,"[52] nor does anyone show greater obedience to nature than when he "according to its orders lets his hands be ready to help."[53]

Nature shows that we differ in form from the rest of the animals. To what end? So that we might understand that we have been endowed with greater surpassing gifts, and that nothing suits us better than to apply ourselves to the duties of gentleness and humaneness. For "we have a natural sense of fidelity, a natural sense of affection, and a natural sense of helpfulness."[54] In fact, has it not "given man two hands, a pair of ears, twin eyes? Why? So that the things that regard the benefit and need of others "might be accomplished more effectively,

---

[46] Lactantius, *De vero cultu* [*Divinarum institutionum libri VII*] 6.10 [FC 49:420].

[47] Lactantius, *De vero cultu* [*Divinarum institutionum libri VII*] 6.11 [FC 49:421].

[48] [Next to this line there is a general reference to] Isa. 58:7.

[49] Seneca, *Epistulae morales* 95.52 [LCL 77:91].

[50] Eph. 5:29.

[51] Ibid.

[52] Seneca, *Epistulae morales* 95.52 [LCL 77:91].

[53] Ibid.

[54] Arrian, *Epicteti dissertationes* 2.10.23 [LCL 131:275].

carefully, and heedfully."[55] Therefore, the less he submits himself to the laws of nature, "the less anyone who does not share with his neighbor the things he needs will be convinced to love that neighbor."[56] In fact, "he who is able to succor one about to perish kills him if he does not give him succor."[57] Therefore, "cherish, as much as you can, and support the souls of men with humaneness lest they be extinguished."[58]

40. The community of society requires us to pursue what is mutually useful, and especially for those we know to be destitute and needy.

Whoever fails to give aid and show favor necessarily removes himself from human society. For this community is such that it cannot exist without beneficence. For why else has it been instituted by God, if not because "man certainly ought to acknowledge man"?[59] Yet this acknowledgment comes when he uses his wealth to help someone he knows to be in need. For that reason, "no one can live happily who has regard to himself alone and transforms everything into a question of his own utility."[60] But for the bond of society to be at its tightest, "each person must live for the other."[61] How great was the force which human society enacted among the heathens? In order to foster and preserve it, they passed up no opportunity to fulfill their duty. Consider Emperor Vespasian, who "was most generous to all classes."[62] As such, he not only avoided the error of avarice, but also obtained a reputation of remarkable generosity. And what should I say of Ptolemy, the king of

---

[55] Cassiodorus, *Variae epistolae* [10.3; Barnish 131; taken from Lang, *Loci communes*, 550r (s.v. *societas*)].

[56] Gregory, *Homiliae in Evangelia* 1.20.11.

[57] Seneca, *De beneficiis* [actually Lactantius, *Divinarum institutionum libri VII* 6.11; FC 49:423].

[58] Lactantius, *De vero cultu* [*Divinarum institutionum libri VII*] 6.11 [FC 49:423].

[59] Lactantius, [*Divinarum institutionum libri VII*] 6.10 [FC 49:420].

[60] Seneca, *Epistulae morales* 48.2 [LCL 75:315].

[61] Ibid.

[62] Suetonius, [*De vita Caesarum (Vespasianus)*] 8.1; LCL 38:297].

the Egyptians? He "hurt none and showed kindness to all, and thus earned himself the name of 'Benefactor.'"[63] So too we ought to be persuaded that "we have a natural fellowship with one another, and that we ought by all means to maintain and guard it."[64] We do this if we "will to benefit our fellow men—many if we can, if not, a few; if not a few, those who are nearest."[65]

41. Other clear examples of respecting society (regarding beneficence).

The bond of human society must be protected in every way, and it is not retained more profitably or beautifully than when one person does good to another. Emperor Titus Vespasianus understood this well when he recalled at dinner that he had given nothing to anyone the entire day, and spoke these memorable and commendable words: "My friends, I have lost a day."[66] From his mouth, too, comes this saying: "No one should go away sorrowful from an interview with his emperor."[67] Oh, if only Christians would consider their day lost if they had shown no favors to others! And if only they would consider it right not to turn away a single needy or sorrowful person! And if "making oneself friendly to the congregation of the poor"[68] was a great preoccupation of the emperor, it should be the same for Christians. "It is worthy of great praise, when man treats man with kindness and generosity."[69]

---

[63] Alexander of Alexandria, [*Geniales dies* 2.11; possibly taken from Zwinger, *Theatrum vitae humanae*, 3.3, 679].

[64] Arrian, *Epicteti dissertationes* 2.20.8 [LCL 131:363].

[65] Seneca, *De vita beata* [= *De Otio* 3.5; LCL 254:187].

[66] Suetonius, [*De vita Caesarum (Divus Titus)* 8.2; LCL 38:317].

[67] *Sabel. lib. 8. c. 2. ex Suida* [= Marcus Antonius Coccius Sabellicus, *Enneades sive Rhapsodia historiarum*, 8.2. The reference to Suidas seems to be incorrect, which can be corrected to Suetonius, *De vita Caesarum (Divus Titus)* 8.2; LCL 38:317].

[68] Sir. 4:[7].

[69] Seneca, [*Epistulae morales* 95.51; LCL 77:91].

The prince of the philosophers, too, was so wise as to perceive this. When he was scolded for giving alms to an impious person, he said, "It was the man and not his character that I considered." Or, as others report, "It was not the man that I assisted but the human race."[70] For this reason, it is a shameful thing when Christians examine the lives of the poor so carefully that, in order to avoid giving to the wicked, they often refuse to give even to their fellow members of Christ, using the indignity of others as a cloak to cover their avarice. "Why do you select persons; why look into the members? You must regard whoever asks of you as a man, since he thinks that you are a man."[71]

Look at the others who were mindful of this social life. Louis the Pious, the king of Germania, "showed piety, benevolence, and generosity."[72] And what Christian conduct did Emperor Frederick IV show when he allowed the bond of society to guide him into doing well? "With his own hand he often gave alms to the poor."[73] Well then, I have considered great men so that you might understand all the better how beautiful it is to excel in this duty of munificence. Therefore, be as benevolent to others as you can. "Give to everyone as circumstances permit."[74] "One's purse should not be closed so tightly that a generous impulse cannot open it,"[75] but it should be opened. For beneficence is not just the bond of Christian society, but those who show themselves generous and beneficent to the poor will also earn themselves the benevolence of God and the love of the pious.

---

[70] Diogenes Laertius, *Vitae philosophorum* (Aristotle) 5.1.17, 21 [LCL 184:461, 465].

[71] Lactantius, *De vero cultu* [*Divinarum institutionum libri VII*] 6.11 [FC 49:423].

[72] Joannes Aventinus, *Annalium boiarum* [(Basel, 1615), 264].

[73] Rahewin, [*Gesta Frederici imperatoris*] 4.80 [perhaps taken from Matthias Flacius Illyricus, *Duodecima centuria ecclesiae historicae* (Basel, 1569), 996].

[74] Cicero, *De officiis* 2 [actually paraphrasing 2.42, 44; LCL 30:47–49].

[75] Cicero, *De officiis* 2 [2.55; LCL 30:225].

7

Eradicate the Evil of Greed

42. The seventh duty of piety consists in bridling the insatiable cupidity for possession. First is shown what this cupidity is, and whom it possesses most of all.

Since all who greedily apply themselves to the cupidity of acquiring wealth are quick to abandon the form of justice and are contemptuous of the pursuit of beneficence, we do well to consider how the evil of greed might be removed from the human mind. The word "avarice" "is φιλαργυρία in Greek. It is not to be understood merely in terms of silver, from which the Greek term is more properly derived, but in regard to everything that is desired immoderately whenever anyone simply wants more than is sufficient. Such avarice is cupidity, and cupidity is a perverse will."[1] If the mind is not kept free of greed, "it becomes unsatisfied whatever its profit, and will not be content even with mountains of gold, but will be forever scrounging to increase its previous gains."[2] It clings to "those brought up in wealth,"[3] "whom

---

[1] Augustine, *De libero arbitrio* 3.17 [FC 59:209–10].

[2] Apuleius, *Apology* 1.20 [LCL 534:59].

[3] Apuleius, *Apology* 1.18 [LCL 534:55].

insatiate hunger and thirst for money possess."[4] For "the more human nature has, the more it desires."[5]

Yet it is the offspring of Mercury that make themselves particularly guilty of this disease since they, "deceived by blind desire,"[6] are accustomed to "imitate the greedy Chalcidians."[7] In fact, "neither burning heat, nor winter, fire, sea, sword, can turn them aside from greed—nothing stops him, until no other man be richer than him."[8] Nor was it without reason that the Thebans had a law forbidding "in government anyone who had not abstained from trading for the last ten years."[9] For they saw no more common vice than greed among the merchants, and that there is no more repulsive evil in particular for those who govern the republic. For "to exploit the state for selfish profit is not only immoral; it is also criminal and infamous."[10] Therefore, let us warn them to "run from greed as a deadly disease which weakens the fiber of virtue."[11]

43. Greed is the first spring from which all vices are born.

Merchants should shun greed, which lies concealed under many kinds of evil. It hinders the one in whom it is, and "when greed has someone in its power, that person shows himself to be subject to all kinds of evil. For it is from greed that all kinds of evil are born and that the

---

[4] Horace, *Epistulae* 1.18 [LCL 194:371].

[5] Marcus Junianus Justinus, [*Historiarum ex Pompeio Trogo lib. XLIIII*] 6.1.

[6] Horace, *Satirae* 1.1 [LCL 194:9].

[7] Caelius Rhodiginus, *Lectiones antiquae* 20.23 [cf. CWE 34:240].

[8] Horace, *Satirae* 1.1 [LCL 194:7].

[9] Aristotle, *Politica* 1278a25 [taken from Alexander of Alexandria, *Geniales dies* 4.6].

[10] Cicero, *De officiis* 2.77 [LCL 30:253].

[11] Ambrose, *De officiis ministrorum* 1.9.193 [Davidson 230].

compulsion to every sin arises."[12] This is why it can rightly be called "a root of all kinds of evil."[13] If you want to consider the evils coming from this malicious root in detail, you will see that it robs people of their humanity. For where greed prevails, "there all good qualities are of little account: honesty, uprightness, a sense of shame, chastity."[14] "Neither training, nor any mental power is strong enough to prevent the mind from submitting more or less quickly, but inevitably."[15] It corrupts judgment, banishing the desire for justice from it. For "there is no trace of justice in those in whom greed has made its dwelling place."[16]

Why do you stand amazed at this? It is "that worst poison of an honest heart, self-interest."[17] It "makes people do and suffer anything, and has abandoned steep virtue's path."[18] This is why there is no such thing as friendship in the kingdom of greed, but "it is the richest nourishment and a spur to every kind of crime: once it establishes itself in a person's mind, it banishes friendship from it."[19] For "he who hastens to

---

[12] [From the high medieval period onward, commonly, but erroneously, attributed to] Augustine, *De libero arbitrio* [no doubt taken from Lang, *Loci communes*, 71r (s.v. *avaritia*); the same passage appears in Gregory the Great's commentary on 1 Tim. 6:10, ch. 9].

[13] 1 Tim. 6:[10].

[14] Sallust, *Epistulae ad Caesarem senem de re publica* [2.8; LCL 522:511].

[15] Sallust, *Epistulae ad Caesarem senem de re publica* [2.4; LCL 522:509–11].

[16] Pope Leo, *Sermones* [*on the Passion of the Lord* 9; the same attribution can be found, for example, in Laurentius Arnoldus, *Collationis philosophiae moralis cum iure scripto* (s.l., 1601), 203].

[17] Tacitus, *Historiae* 1.15 [LCL 111:31].

[18] Horace, *Carmina* 3.24 [LCL 33:201].

[19] Baptista Fulgosus, [*De dictis factisque memorabilibus collectanea a Camillo Gilino latina facta* (Milan, 1509)], 9.4 [possibly taken from Bartholomaus Amantius, *Flores celebriorum sententiarum Graecarum ac Latinarum* (s.l., 1566), 56 (s.v. *avaritia*)].

be rich also looks maliciously at others."[20] Yet greed not only corrupts, but also destroys all things. "Wherever it goes, it devastates towns, the countryside, shrines, and homes. No army and no fortifications stop it from forcing its way through."[21] "Gold has a way of passing through the middle of bodyguards, and breaking through rocks more effectively than a stroke of lightning."[22] "O greed, you wicked pest! All upright minds should hate you! Do you leave anything unhurt and unchanged? You threw the human race into disarray, excluded a disciple and follower of Christ from apostleship, and took the soldiers guarding the tomb captive."[23]

Greed is an untamed and monstrous beast that no mind should tolerate, since "the sin of avarice makes the mind it infects so heavy that it can never desire to be lifted up to the heights."[24] "So it happens that the poor and lowly who are unimpeded believe in God more easily than the rich who are surrounded with many impediments of greed. Rather, indeed, they are chained and shackled in their service to the wish of their mistress, desire, which has them caught in inextricable bonds. Nor can they look toward heaven, because their mind is turned toward earth and fastened on the ground."[25] And so, O vice of vices, villainy of villainies, and crime of crimes! Who would not shrink back or flee from you? For you are so malicious that, once all virtues have dissipated, you beget and bear all vices!

---

[20] Prov. 28:20.

[21] Sallust, *Epistulae ad Caesarem senem de re publica* [2.4; LCL 522:513].

[22] Horace, *Carmina* 3.16 [LCL 33:183].

[23] Rabanus Maurus, *Expositio in Matthaeum* [6; possibly taken from Antonius Rampelogus, *Figurae bibliae* (Lyon, 1554), 65].

[24] Gregory, *Moralia in Iob* 14.53.63 [Kerns 3:187; probably taken from Lang, *Loci communes*, 72v (s.v. *avaritia*)].

[25] Lactantius, *De divino praemio* [*Divinarum institutionum libri VII*] 7.1 [FC 49:473].

44. Contentment (αὐτάρκεια) should be placed over against extravagant cupidity for riches.

We described in part the evils that closely follow greed. Will anyone still pursue it? And you, do you still pursue it, showing that you prefer to set your wealth in the greedy accumulation of riches rather than contentment (αὐτάρκεια) and self-sufficiency? "You poor fellow! What a Charybdis you are caught in!"[26] Do you not know? "Those who seek a lot lack a lot. All is well for the man to whom God with a frugal hand has given enough."[27] "Indeed, in life as in swimming you are all the better for being free of burdens, for just as in this storm of human life, what is light buoys you up, what is heavy drags you down."[28] "The way of beatitude therefore does not admit those bearing great burdens."[29] But happier are those who "are more inclined to disciplined moderation,"[30] and richer are those who want less "by controlling their greedy spirit."[31] Why then do you pursue wealth so greedily? "Esteem your fortune as a tunic, for its propriety not for its excess."[32] "Better is the poor who walks in his integrity than one perverse in his ways, though he be rich."[33] Believe me, you will only appease your mind with peaceful tranquility and protect it from every storm of vices if you, "swift to punish dishonest greed and aloof from money that draws everything into its embrace,"[34] subdue the desires

---

[26] Horace, *Carmina* 1.27 [LCL 33:75].

[27] Horace, *Carmina* 3.16 [LCL 33:187].

[28] Apuleius, *Apologia (Pro se de magia)* 1.21 [LCL 534:61; trans. note: I read *tempestate* for *tempestates*].

[29] Lactantius, *De divino praemio* [*Divinarum institutionum libri VII*] 7.1 [FC 49:473].

[30] Apuleius, *Apologia (Pro se de magia)* 1.19 [LCL 534:57].

[31] Horace, *Carmina* 2.2 [LCL 33:101].

[32] Apuleius, *Apologia (Pro se de magia)* 1.19 [LCL 534:57].

[33] Prov. 19:[1] [and Prov. 28:6, which contains the second clause].

[34] Horace, *Carmina* 4.9 [LCL 33:247].

of your mind. Therefore, flee the great and return to the small. Then "you will live wisely, if cheerful in your lot."[35]

45. Riches are to be had without greed.

My intention is not to take riches and other goods away from Christians altogether, since "they depend on the attitude of those who possess them; they are good for those who know how to enjoy them, bad for those who do not enjoy them properly."[36] For that reason, it is to be held that "guilt is not in the goods themselves, but in those who know not how to use them. For just as riches are impediments to virtue in the greedy, so they are means of aid for virtue to the good."[37] See to it, therefore, that your mind is not shackled by greed. How? "There are spells and sayings whereby you may soothe the pain and cast much of the malady aside."[38] Hear the counsel given by a sacred king: "If riches increase, do not set your heart on them."[39] The heart is set on them when the mind full of insatiable greed cannot check riches, and when "shameless wealth continues to grow, yet there is always something missing, making the fortune incomplete."[40] To know how illicit it really is, hear these words from our only Savior's mouth: "Take heed and beware of greed," says Christ, "for one's life does not consist in the abundance of the things he possesses."[41] Hear also the pious voice of the apostle: "Godliness with contentment is great gain."[42] You will achieve this if you "aim at a fixed limit for your desires"[43] and

---

[35] Horace, *Epistulae* 1.10 [LCL 194:319].

[36] Terence, *Hauton Timorumenos* 1.2 [LCL 22:199].

[37] Ambrose, *Expositio Evangelii secundum Lucam* [8; MPL 15:1791; taken from Lang, *Loci communes*, 179r (s.v. *divitiae*)].

[38] Horace, *Epistulae* 1.1 [LCL 194:253].

[39] Ps. 62:10.

[40] Horace, [*Carmina*] 3.24 [LCL 33:201].

[41] Luke 12:15.

[42] 1 Tim. 6:6.

[43] Horace, *Epistulae* 1.1 [LCL 194:267].

your "conduct shall be without greed."[44] For "better is the little that a righteous man has than the many riches of a greedy man."[45]

46. The examples of those who offered powerful resistance to the greedy desires of their minds. Everyone ought to be like them.

What? Is "your bosom still fevered with avarice and sordid covetousness"?[46] May these examples of virtues move you "because they creep into the mind with powerful authority."[47]

First, what self-control was shown by the sacred patriarch Jacob! Spurning the riches of the world, he only asked God for "bread to eat and clothing to put on."[48] And what did God give him? "In the time between, the Lord God heaped upon him so much honor and wealth that nothing seems to be lacking to complete his happiness."[49] Indeed, "the more a person denies himself, the more he will receive from God."[50]

Second, what greatness of mind was shown by Saint Peter! Although Simon Magus offered him money, it failed to move his mind. "He placed honor before convenience, rejected the bribes of the guilty with a disdainful look, and carried his weapons victoriously through the hosts that were ranged against him."[51] Peter said to him, "Your money perish with you, because you thought that the gift of God could be purchased with money!"[52]

And, third, what should I say of that famous tax collector called Matthew? At one time he indeed burned with greed and an insatiable

---

[44] Heb. 13:5.

[45] Sir. 36; 14:2 [actually Ps. 37:16].

[46] Horace, *Epistulae* 1.1 [LCL 194:253].

[47] Juvenal, *Satirae* 14 [LCL 91:461].

[48] Gen. 28:20.

[49] Tacitus, *Annales* 14.53 [LCL 322:191].

[50] Horace, *Carmina* 3.16 [LCL 33:185].

[51] Horace, *Carmina* 4.9 [LCL 33:247].

[52] Acts 8:20.

thirst for wealth. But see, when the Lord Jesus Christ called him, he "left his tax office."[53] And "destitute himself, he wants to join the camp of those who desire nothing; a deserter, he is eager to abandon the side of the rich, and thus acquire more credit for being master of the wealth he rejects."[54]

Fourth, consider similarly the lives of other great and godly men, and you will see that they remained unmoved by desire for earthly riches. For all these earthly goods "they always accounted transient and fleeting, the bestowal not of virtue and genius but of circumstance. It was not so much opportunities for acquiring and amassing these that they thought desirable, but rather calculation in their enjoyment and steadfastness in their loss."[55]

Therefore, O Christian, having become wiser by these examples, "you ought to cherish the golden mean."[56] "The one who has the least desires will have the most, since by wanting the least he will have all he wants."[57] "For he is not poor, who has enough of things to use."[58] A modest home offers no small happiness as well as "a sense of freedom from care without which nothing is pleasant."[59] To obtain it, "with hands upturned to the sky,"[60] follow the example of the royal prophet and say to God, "Incline my heart to your testimonies, and not to covetousness. Turn away my eyes from looking at worthless things, and revive me in your way."[61]

---

[53] Matt. 9:[10].

[54] Horace, *Carmina* 3.16 [LCL 33:185].

[55] Cicero, *De domo sua* [LCL 158:309].

[56] Horace, *Carmina* 2.10 [LCL 33:115].

[57] Apuleius, *Apologia (Pro se de magia)* 1.20 [LCL 534:59].

[58] Horace, *Epistulae* 1.12 [LCL 194:329].

[59] Seneca, *Epistulae morales* 20.12 [LCL 75:139].

[60] Horace, *Carmina* 3.23 [LCL 33:195].

[61] Ps. 119:36–37.

8

Cut Off the Destructive Thorns of Worry

47. The eighth duty of piety is to throw off all destructive worries weighing heavily on the children of wealth.

Greed also has pernicious companions, namely, anxious worries. However, it is Satan's work "to give the rich worries and anxieties about temporal matters, so that they consider necessary what is neither necessary nor a matter of life and death."[1] He gladly besieges their minds with such worries to hinder them, "so that they never want to consider anything that offers security or have the strength to desire it."[2] Accordingly, many of them "have numerous paralyzing worries weighing down their breast."[3] In fact, this punishment is so deadly that countless cares torment the hearts of those who have many possessions. This was recognized by Anacreon of Teos who lay sleepless for two nights after receiving two talents from Polycrates, the tyrant of Samos. He returned them to him and said, "I consider them to be unworthy of such care."[4] It is as though he had said, "I lie awake half-dead with fear, to be in terror of night and day of wicked thieves, of

---

[1] Thomas Stapleton, *Promptuarium morale* [could not be found].

[2] Thomas Stapleton, *Promptuarium morale* [could not be found].

[3] Plautus, *Rudens* [221; LCL 260:425].

[4] Lilius Gregorius Gyraldus, *Poetarum historia*, [*graecorum et latinorum* (Basel, 1545), 1006].

fire, of slaves, who may rob me and run away—is this so pleasant? In such blessings I could wish ever to be poorest of the poor."[5]

Emperor Sigismund experienced the same torment of cares in the possession of riches. When forty thousand gold coins were brought to him from Hungary, "at nightfall he anxiously began to think of the uses to which he might put that money."[6] Thus he discovered that "wakefulness over wealth wastes away one's flesh, and anxiety about it drives away sleep."[7] For this reason, he quickly had a chamber servant summon his advisors and military commanders. After opening the chest he said, "These (showing the coins) are the cruel adversaries and tormenters that have deprived me of my sleep. Take these and divide them amongst yourselves, so that I can sleep peacefully."[8] When the money had been divided and the men began to leave the meeting, he said, "Now the tormentor that scourged me is going away, and I will sleep more soundly."[9] This is why I may now shout aloud: "O marvelous blessedness of mortal riches! When you have gained that blessedness, you have lost your security."[10] So riches that are otherwise taken as a good degenerate into a torment and rack for their owners.

48. How heavily merchants are weighed down by their worries.

The Romans used to have "people wasted by sorrows" (*curiones*) named after the "sorrows" (*curis*) that made them so thin. But why should we consider them? We will consider our "people wasted by sorrows," and those involved in business, seeing "how many concerns weigh them

---

[5] Horace, *Satirae* 1.1 [LCL 194:11].

[6] Johannes Cuspianus, [prb. *De Caesaribus et Imperatoribus*]; Aeneas Sylvius Piccolomini, *Commentarius in orationem Alphonsi regis*, [in *Opera* (Basel, 1571), 493].

[7] Sir. 31:1.

[8] Johannes Cuspianus, [prb. *De Caesaribus et Imperatoribus*]; Aeneas Sylvius Piccolomini, *Commentarius in orationem Alphonsi regis*, [in *Opera*, 493].

[9] Ibid.

[10] Boethius, *De consolatione philosophiae* 2.5 [LCL 74:207].

down and pull their heart in different directions!"[11] "They outdo and surpass everyone in mental agony. They are being thrown around, tossed around, pierced, turned on the wheel of the world—poor them. They are being destroyed, driven, driven apart, dragged apart, torn apart: so clouded is their mind. Where they are, there they are not, where they are not, there is their heart."[12] "Today," they say, "or tomorrow we will go to such and such a city, spend a year there, buy and sell, and make a profit."[13] Afterwards, "they wear out their brains with ever changing plans."[14] For the merchant's will includes also this: "Goading those enjoying it, and like swarming bees that have poured out their pleasing honey, it flees, and strikes hearts with a too lasting sting."[15] Allow me, however, to offer a remedy to this ailment, "dispelling the worries that gnaw the heart."[16] First, I will show that these worries are to be thrown off for their malicious powers and ruinous poison.

49. On the harm and destructive powers of worries.

Anyone who feeds the destructive worries within finds himself surrounded by dangerous and enraged enemies. For anxieties are thorns "that not only do not bear eternal fruit but even hinder those who wish to gain it. Thorns are the food of irrational camels; they are devoured and consumed by fire, being useful for nothing. Such are destructive worries, useful for nothing, but to kindle the furnace, to light up the Day that burns as an oven, to nourish passions void of reason."[17]

If you consider what they do, you will see that they are very damaging to the soul. First, because they darken the light of the mind:

---

[11] Terence, *Andria* [260; LCL 22:75].

[12] Plautus, *Cistellaria* [205–11; LCL 61:155].

[13] James 4:13.

[14] Horace, *Carmina* 2.11 [LCL 33:117].

[15] Boethius, *De consolatione philosophiae* 3.6 [LCL 74:259].

[16] Horace, *Carmina* 1.18 [LCL 33:61].

[17] John Chrysostom, *Homiliae in epistulam ii ad Thessalonicenses* 3 [NPNF1 13:387; possibly taken from Jean Dadré, *Loci communes similium et dissimilium ex omni propemodum*, (Cologne, 1594), 185r-v (s.v. *divitiae, dives*)].

"For just like the eye of the body cannot clearly perceive an object put before it while it is wandering restless up and down and sideways, without fixing a steady gaze upon it, so a mind distracted by six hundred worldly cares is hardly able clearly to perceive the truth."[18]

Second, worries make piety very difficult: "For as the sun is clear and shown publicly before all, and we have no need to seek it; but if, on the other hand, we bury ourselves and turn everything upside down, we need much labor to see the sun—so also if we bury and entangle ourselves completely in the cares of worldly affairs, we have difficulty lifting our eyes to behold with our mind the light of grace and truth and salvation which is shown to all."[19]

Finally, anxieties slowly wear out the soul and devour it. "For just like a vine produces its own root and sprouts from itself, but then grows by wrapping itself tightly around the tree next to it, and after wrapping itself around that tree reaches upwards by the aid and support of the latter; but then so chokes it by its embrace and holds it so tightly that it no longer receives sap and cannot sprout, and thus necessarily dies as if its life has been choked out from it—so, too, the cares for or worry about earthly things first uses the work and efforts of the soul to acquire earthly things, but later covers the soul and entangles it, so that the soul suffocates and stumbles under the weight, no longer able to aspire to heavenly things."[20] For this reason, the fortress of anxieties is to be torn down, and these tyrants cast out. For you will be performing a great duty of piety and virtue if you cut off unnecessary cares and misguided worries.

---

[18] Basil, *Epistulae* 1 [NPNF2 8:110; this and the following five quotations are taken from Thomas Stapleton, *Promptuarium morale ... pars aestivalis* (Antwerp, 1593), resp. from 330, 333, and 327].

[19] John Chrysostom, *Homiliae in epistulam ad Hebraeos* 22 [NPNF1 14:468].

[20] Hector Pinto, *Imagine della vita christiana overo Dialoghi morali Hector Pinto* [(Venice, 1595, 6.1.4. Cf. *Opera latina omnia IV* (Lyon, 1584), 96. The Portugese edition lacks the part divisions and does not number the dialogs, and the Lyon *Opera* edition provides a Latin text different from Souterius's.]

50. That worries are to be eradicated from the soul is taught by Christ's admonition in Matthew 6:25: "Do not worry."

How radically the worries of this life are to be rooted out from the soul is taught by our Redeemer when he says, "Therefore I say to you, do not worry."[21] In the same chapter, he impresses these words upon us no less than three times. What does he mean by them? "By this command God wants us not to be overly worried, and rather to trust in the Lord."[22] Indeed, "work is to be done, and anxiety is to be taken away."[23] Therefore, "nothing is being reproved here except excessive worry. He did not say that you should not sow (or conduct business), but that from now on you ought not to be worried or anxious. He also does not say that you ought not to work, but that you ought not to be fainthearted and filled with the trouble of your cares."[24]

First, you should not conduct yourself like those who resemble pigs and care for nothing but their fodder. "For to all of you that concern yourselves with property, lands, slaves (and other earthly things)—they are anxious about nothing but fodder!"[25] What a worry full of foolishness is this! Do you think God has put us in the world "to be anxious only about our wretched body and trifling estate, but to care nothing for the things that are within us"?[26]

Second, if you do think so, let me examine the illness of your mind. Just like it is "by a person's color that a physician judges that he is acting from his spleen,"[27] so I from the color and warmth of your perverse inclination and foolish appetite will say that you are exerting yourself in vain. Accordingly, for the sake of your salvation it will be

---

[21] Matt. 6:25.

[22] Basil, [*Regulis brevioribus*], interr. 207.

[23] Jerome, *Com. de serm. Domini in monte* [actually *Commentariorium in Matthaeum*] 2.6.

[24] Augustine, *Homil. in Matth.* 22 [actually Chrysostom, *Homiliae in Matthaeum*].

[25] Arrian, *Epicteti dissertationes* 2.14.25 [LCL 131:305].

[26] Arrian, *Epicteti dissertationes* 2.13.11 [LCL 131:293].

[27] Arrian, *Epicteti dissertationes* 2.13.12 [LCL 131:293].

better for you to listen once more to the warning given by your Lord: "Therefore do not worry about tomorrow, for tomorrow will worry about its own things. Sufficient for the day is its own trouble."[28] Do you hear these things, O merchant? "So put aside that false worry which is tormenting you."[29]

51. Another argument for casting off the soul's petty anxieties drawn from the brevity of this life.

Next, "think at the same time about how short life is."[30] Is it not shameful and embarrassing "to worry about provisions when you only have a short way to go"?[31] Is it not a foolish cupidity when it compels you in this short span of life "to have tastes beyond your wallet"?[32] How great the mind of Crates has been! Pondering the brevity of life, "he threw over everything for a single stick, and exchanged his well-furnished country houses for a single sack,"[33] lest he sink under his anxious worries. I wish that all Christians would show the same mind, seeking nothing except what they need for their household. That is, that they might cast off the thorns of worries and, "having food and clothing, be content with these."[34] If anyone wants to learn this true philosophy, he should reflect upon "how small a part of life it is that we really live."[35]

What is man? "Man is a dream of a shadow."[36] What is human life? "Men are short-lived."[37] "This our life is a daily passage from life: every

---

[28] Matt. 6:34.

[29] Terence, *Hauton timorumenos* [177; LCL 22:195].

[30] Plautus, *Mostellaria* [725; LCL 163:389].

[31] Seneca [could not be found].

[32] Erasmus, *Adagia*, [3.5.62; CWE 35:103].

[33] Apuleius, *Apologia (Pro se de magia)* 1.22 [LCL 534:63].

[34] 1 Tim. 6:8.

[35] Seneca, [*De brevitate vitae* 2.2; LCL 254:291].

[36] Josephus, in Lang, *Loci communes* [could not be found; the original source is Plutarch, *Moralia* (Letter to Apollonius) 104B; LCL 222:121].

[37] Homer, *Odyssea* 19 l. 328 [LCL 105:259].

day a little of our life is taken from us; even when we are growing, our life is on the wane."[38] More than that, "the further life advances, the closer it approaches death."[39] What is our state? "Like the grass of midsummer, it lives for a short time: in an instant it springs up, in an instant it withers away."[40] For that reason, it might be said as truly as elegantly that "the very day which we are now spending is shared between ourselves and death."[41] What use is it therefore "to spend the greater part of this time, which is so short and swift and carries us away in its flight, on useless things"?[42] "Oh, why do we spend the years of our lives in worry, tormenting ourselves with fears and senseless desires; grown old before our time with anxieties which never end; wasting our lives in the pursuit of gain; setting no limit to our wishes, so that their fulfillment leaves us still unblest, but ever playing the part of men who mean to live yet never do?"[43]

52. How much the useless worry in human endeavor is to be rejected, demonstrated by the endeavor of the mayfly.

The blindness by which the human race overanxiously hunts up the needs of this short life can readily be demonstrated by the application of the mayfly, which "by the river Hypanis, flowing into the Pontus from a part of Europe, is born and lives for a single day."[44] The mayfly receives its life when the sun rises at dawn and dies in the evening when it sets. "At dawn it is a child, at noon a youth, in the evening an old man. And so it seems that nature devotes more time and labor

---

[38] Seneca, *De brevitate vitae* 2. [Actually the first clause is from Gregory the Great, *Moralia in Iob*, 11.50; and the final one from Seneca, *Epistulae morales*, 24.20; LCL 75:177.]

[39] [Pseudo-]Augustine, *Soliloquia animae ad Deum* 2 [MPL 40:867].

[40] Plautus, *Pseudolus* [38; LCL 260:247].

[41] Seneca, [*Epistulae morales* 24.20; LCL 75:177].

[42] Seneca, [*Epistulae morales* 117.32; LCL 77:359].

[43] Manus Manilius, *Astronomica* 4.1–5 [LCL 469.223].

[44] Plutarch, *Moralia* (Beasts Are Rational) [actually from Cicero, *Tusculanae disputationes* 1.94; LCL 141:113].

to its generation, than to the course of its life."⁴⁵ But what makes the mayfly so admirable is that, "although it lives so short, it still seeks whatever is necessary for that brief life with no less application than if it lived a longer life than all other animals."⁴⁶

Let us now apply these things to our topic. Will a man not laugh at the mayfly's endeavor when he compares the brevity of its life to the long span of his own? And yet, should a man not marvel all the more at the endeavor of the man overcome by worries who, though he lives but a life of an hour, does not "stop gaping at the acquisition of wealth and riches with great care and worry"?⁴⁷ "Yet the time is short,"⁴⁸ and "we have no continuing city here."⁴⁹ And if we compare our life with that of the angels, it proves much shorter even than that of the mayfly. More than that, "contrast our longest lifetime with eternity, [and] it shall be found very short."⁵⁰ Indeed, "in this brief and transitory course of life, what great labors shall a man pursue?"⁵¹ How much does man "fuss about the needs of our short life"?⁵² "For man there is no end to his riches."⁵³ This is why the angels stand amazed at the human race's useless endeavor; everyone should deride these vain worries. As for us, let us rather live a pious life, spurning this earthly squalor and "the form of this world,"⁵⁴ content with our share and free from these cares. Let that small animalcule serve as an example to us, "that tiny, hard-working ant, which drags all she can with her mouth, and adds it

---

⁴⁵ Ludovicus Granatensis, *Sylva locorum communium omnibus Verbi Domini concionaturibus* [(Lyon, 1586), 802].

⁴⁶ Ibid.

⁴⁷ Ibid.

⁴⁸ 1 Cor. 7:29.

⁴⁹ Heb. 13:14.

⁵⁰ Cicero, *Tusculanae disputatationes* 1.94 [LCL 141:113].

⁵¹ Cicero, *Pro Archia* [29; LCL 158:37].

⁵² Horace, *Carmina* 2.11 [LCL 33:117].

⁵³ Bar. 3:17 [in Latin translations of Plutarch's *De cupiditate divitiarum*, 4, this quote is attributed to Solon, no doubt alluding to Aristotle, *Politica* 1.5].

⁵⁴ 1 Cor. 7:31.

to the heap she is building,"⁵⁵ and "which takes the tops off the grains she has collected so that they do not germinate in the soil or decay. In this she shows her prudence."⁵⁶ So, too, we ought to put to death the seeds of worry in us, so that the underlying growth does not by our negligence and empty cares become poisonous fruit that may kill us.

53. An argument against human worries drawn from the fatherly providence of God.

In order that a merchant might be more eager to tear out the spines of worry, he should consider the providence of God, which governs all things, to which all things are subject, and "by whose will and command the nations' lands are governed."⁵⁷ If someone acknowledges this providence, will he not also confess being governed by it? And how would he say that he is governed by it, unless he also believes that it looks out for him? You who are so full of cares and worries—what are the things that cause you to weigh everything so anxiously, and of what kind are they? Are they necessary? Or are they unnecessary and superfluous? Regardless what you answer, I will prove the vanity of what you are doing. Do you seek things that are not necessary? This is no wonder, since it is divine providence that sees to it and ensures that you do not have them, because you are seeking burdens that will only weigh you down and even bring about your end. "Indeed with all things that we use for the tasks of life, anything that exceeds proper limits is an excrescence more burdensome than useful."⁵⁸ And "just as fruitfulness and excessive luxury kills certain trees, so extravagant enjoyment of things ruins some of us."⁵⁹ What was it that killed the

---

55 Horace, *Satirae* 1.1 [LCL 194:7].

56 Bonaventure, *Dieta salutis* 5.5.

57 [Pseudo-]Cicero, *Ad populum et equites Romanos antequam erit in exilium* 10.

58 Apuleius, *Apologia (Pro se de magia)* 1.19 [LCL 534:57].

59 Erasmus, [*Parabolae, sive similitudines, ex Aristotele, Theophrasto, Plutarcho, Plinio ac Seneca* (Frankfurt, 1568), 99; perhaps taken from Lang, *Loci communes*, 390v (s.v. *mediocritas*)].

rich Epulon? The abundance of things by which he was, as it were, "burdened with many huge packs, and advanced upon the way of death."[60] For that reason, you need to commit yourself freely to providence, which "guides the reins of your things"[61] and "in its foresight keeps you unharmed"[62] when your desire is excessive.

But perhaps you will rather say that you are seeking things that are necessary for life. But I will argue from this that you need not be worried about these things for the very reason that they are necessary. "For the Lord has said, 'I will never leave you nor forsake you.'"[63] "Fear the Lord, you his saints! Those who seek the Lord shall not lack any good thing."[64] Therefore, "what you consider a cause for being anxious, this I say suffices to free you from your anxiety. For if you say, 'I have reason to worry because they are necessary,' I will respond, 'You need not worry because they are necessary.' But if they were superfluous, you ought not to place your trust in them. But since they are necessary, you should no longer doubt."[65]

54. The fatherly care of God, by which he watches all men and especially the people who are his own, also acts against the worries of the world.

If you consider God the giver and father of all, why are you afraid that you will lack life's shelter and gifts? "There is one Father of all things, one who looks after all."[66] Consider also the following: "If a son asks for bread from any father among you, will he give him a stone? If you, then, being evil, know how to give good gifts to your children, how much more will your heavenly Father give the Holy Spirit to

---

[60] Lactantius, *De divino praemio* [*Divinarum institutionum libri VII*] 7.1 [FC 49:473].

[61] Boethius, [*De consolatione philosophiae*] 3.2 [LCL 74:237].

[62] Ibid.

[63] Heb. 13:6.

[64] Ps. 34:9–10.

[65] Chrysostom, *Homiliae in Matthaeum* 23 [NPNF1 10:149].

[66] Boethius, [*De consolatione philosophiae*] 3.6 [LCL 74:257].

those who ask him!"⁶⁷ Just as "the welfare of the people is the highest law"⁶⁸ to the fathers of the fatherland, so the greatest care of God, the world's Maker and the heavenly Father, is to those to whom he is a father. Why, then, do you "spend the chilly nights sleepless and wretched because of your many troubles"?⁶⁹ O wretched man! How blind you are, and how blinded your eyes, so that you fail to see the fount and Father of the lights, "from whom comes down every good gift and every perfect gift from above"⁷⁰ and to whom you can safely entrust yourself! Let us consider how much he cares for you. "Birds lack nothing, and cattle live on day by day; for wild beasts their solitude suffices for nourishment."⁷¹ If God shows such care for the whole world, will you be the only one he overlooks? "Look at the birds of the air, for they neither sow nor reap nor gather into barns; yet your heavenly Father feeds them. Are you not of more value than they?"⁷² Therefore, "do not worry."⁷³

55. To ward off worries, an argument is drawn from these words of the apostle in Acts 17:28: "For we are also his offspring."

Anyone with some connection to God has no reason to murmur, "Who will give us meat to eat?"⁷⁴ Nor should he worry and cry out, "Where shall we buy bread, that we may eat?"⁷⁵ Instead, he has every reason to lay down and put off his gloomy worries since some kinship binds him to God. "For we are also his offspring."⁷⁶ "He also peopled

---

⁶⁷ Luke 11:12–13.

⁶⁸ The Twelve Tables of Roman Law.

⁶⁹ Horace, *Carmina* 3.7 [LCL 33:165; alternative reading].

⁷⁰ James 1:17.

⁷¹ [Pseudo-?]Seneca, *De remediis fortuitorum* [10.1].

⁷² Matt. 6:26.

⁷³ Matt. 6:31.

⁷⁴ Num. 11:4.

⁷⁵ John 6:5.

⁷⁶ Acts 17:28.

the earth with men; he locked into limbs spirits brought down from their high abode. So did a noble seed produce all mortals."[77] Anyone who enjoys such kinship with God, his "mind is happy for the present, and he should refuse to worry about what is further ahead."[78] Indeed, "kinship with Caesar or any other of them that have power will make a person believe that he has enough aid and defense to live securely and free of contempt, and lead him to consider that he will never be destitute of the necessities of life."[79] Now there is indeed a connection and bond between you and God, and "our souls are so bound up with God and joined together with him, since they are his parts and are taken from him."[80] As a result, there is even less reason for any anxiety to press itself upon and squeeze you. For "unless God willed to preserve what is, he would not have created it. Since he himself determined that living beings are to be preserved by food and the body by clothing, he administers them both."[81] Use this argument to fashion and fortify your mind.

56. An argument for warding off worries taken from these words of Peter in 1 Peter 5:7: "Cast all your care upon him."

Let us also consider this judgment full of comfort to the souls by the divine Peter: "Humble yourselves under the mighty hand of God, casting all your care upon him, for he cares for you."[82] Having been encouraged and fortified, we cry out, "The Lord is our help, what shall I fear?"[83] Or, again, we say, "The Lord is our shepherd; we shall not

---

[77] Boethius, [*De consolatione philosophiae*] 3.6 [LCL 74:257].

[78] Horace, *Carmina* 2.16 [LCL 33:129].

[79] Arrian, *Epicteti dissertationes* [1.9.7; LCL 131:65].

[80] Arrian, [*Epicteti dissertationes* 1.14.6; LCL 131:101].

[81] Chrysostom [could not be found; the same attribution can be found in, for example, Johannes Royardus, *Homiliae in evangelia dominicalia* (Lyon, 1573), 171r].

[82] 1 Peter 5:6–7.

[83] Ps. 118:6.

be in need."[84] Why? The servants of earthly lords lack no food—will you, servants whose Lord is the greatest and most high God, then be forsaken? "A good soldier does not lack someone to give him pay, or a workman, or a cobbler; and shall a good man? Does God neglect his own commissioners and servants, and does he show no care for his witnesses?—whom alone he uses as examples to teach the uninstructed that he is Lord and governs the universe well, and that he does not neglect the affairs of men, so that no evil befalls a good man either in life or in death?"[85] Why, then, would he not offer him food also in this life? He is the faithful Lord, who "makes his sun rise on the evil and on the good, and sends rain on the just and on the unjust."[86] He is the Lord, present always and everywhere, who sees to the care of all. He "who observes the steps and paths we take, who watches over people day and night as if oblivious to all else and concerned for them alone—he always shows himself there and prepared, whenever he finds a man prepared. Wherever a man goes the Lord will not fail to be, unless that man first abandons him."[87] Since you cannot exist without this Lord, O worrywart, tell me why you fear that you will be lost with him. "Wherever you may be, he does not withdraw, since he is everywhere, so that wherever you may go, you will find the one through whom you can be."[88] Therefore, always hold him before your eyes, and boldly set him over your anxious worries, so that he "who knows that you need all these things"[89] will supply you with all things, since from him come "all things from which the righteous who love him live."[90]

---

[84] Ps. 23:1.
[85] Arrian, *Epicteti dissertationes* 3.26.27 [LCL 218:233–35].
[86] Matt. 5:45.
[87] [Pseudo-]Augustine, *Soliloquia animae ad Deum* 14 [MPL 40:875].
[88] Ibid.
[89] Matt. 6:32.
[90] [Pseudo-?]Augustine, *Manuale* 4 [MPL 40:954].

57. On the fruits that come when empty worries are cut off.

Let us now consider the fruits. For just as sailors, "when they see land in the distance from the see,"[91] pluck the benefits and fruits of the troubles they endured on the way, let us, who after this short and brief sailing trip reached solid ground and the end of this topic of worries, now treat the fruits that come when worries have been cut off.

First, would you like a life of tranquility? You will have it when "you have removed inconsequential worries from your mind."[92] For as long as worries subdue and will subdue the minds, "they leave no share of rest day or night."[93] But when they are gone, the halcyon delights of untroubled rest and pleasant repose return. I say "rest," since "it repairs the strength of the mind."[94] I say "repose"—"not by jewels or purple or gold or riches. For no consul's lictor can move on the disorders of an unhappy mind and the anxieties that flutter around coffered ceilings. The good life is enjoyed at little expense by the man whose forefathers' saltcellar gleams on his frugal table, one who is not robbed of his blithe slumbers by fear of sordid greed."[95]

Next, what greater good might one expect? Indeed, if the turmoil of worries is removed from the house of your mind, you, who up to now have lived only for yourself and your empty cares, will start living for the other, that is, your neighbor. For anyone who is burdened by these things does not turn his thoughts to the affairs of others. But "with the harper of Aspendus he makes 'all the music inside.'"[96] But freed of cares, "he is a friendly companion, obliging to all, burdensome to none, devoted to God, friendly to his neighbor, temperate to the world; he is the Lord's servant, a companion to one's neighbor, lord of

---

[91] Plautus, *Menaechmi* [228; LCL 61:451].

[92] Gregory, *Moralia in Iob* 2.52.82 [Kerns 1:182; probably taken with adaptation from Lang, *Loci communes*, 111v (s.v. *cogitatio*)].

[93] Cicero, *Pro Cluentio* [actually *De Lege agraria* 2.5; LCL 240:375].

[94] Ovid, *Heroides* 90 [LCL 41:51].

[95] Horace, *Carmina* 2.16 [LCL 33:129].

[96] Cicero, *In Verrem* 2.53 [LCL 221:177; i.e., for one's own pleasure and not that of others].

the world: he has his upper parts for joy, middle parts for fellowship, lower parts for service."[97]

Finally, I want a mind free from the disturbances of worry, not in order that it may live recklessly and slothfully like a pig from the sty of Epicurus,[98] but as if the mind, "deprived from anxiety, begins to open up to joy,"[99] and being more free may direct itself to the contemplation of the divine. "Our mind is not led to internal contemplation in any other way than by carefully extricating itself from clinging occupations. Our mind is absolutely not caught up into the road[100] of interior contemplation unless it is first diligently lulled to sleep against the clamor of earthly desires."[101] This fruit is readily perceived by anyone who refuses to be bound by the chains of worry. The contemplation of the divine "enraptures every soul with the desire of it, and the more ardent it is the purer it is, and the purer it is the more it rises to spiritual things, and the more it rises to spiritual things the more it dies to material things."[102] Since the welfare of the soul and the sight of beauty are partly established in it, it will not be out of place for us to encourage and incite all minds to it at greater length soon afterwards in what follows.[103]

---

[97] Hugo of St. Victor, *De anima* 3; Bernard of Clairvaux, *Meditationes de humana conditione* 4.13 [MPL 184:494; these two works of Hugo and Bernard have a convoluted textual history; see MPL 177:165–66].

[98] [This is an allusion to Horace, *Epistulae* 1.4; LCL 194:277.]

[99] Tacitus, *Histories* 1.44 [LCL 111:73].

[100] [Trans. note: Gregory's *Moralia in Iob* actually reads *vim* ("power") here (MPL 75:710), but for this translation I read *viam* ("road") after Souterius, who takes this reading from Lang's *Loci communes*; see the next note.]

[101] Gregory, *Moralia in Iob* 5.31.55 [Kerns 3:355–56; taken from Lang, *Loci communes*, 112v (s.v. *cogitatio*)].

[102] Augustine, *De Trinitate* [2.28; FC 45:86].

[103] [See especially ch. 9, section 71.]

9

DESPISE THE LOVE OF EARTHLY THINGS AND STRIVE FOR HEAVENLY THINGS

58. *The ninth duty of piety is located in the pursuit of heavenly things. First, we treat those who want to serve two lords: God, by seeking what is of heaven; and the world, by loving what is of the earth.*

Before we conclude this work, we need to speak about the pursuit of the highest good of all heavenly things. For it is the foremost work of piety and the chief of all others. If a merchant directs his mind to it, he deserves to be called truly wise and truly blessed. This is why our heavenly teacher rightly gave the following encouragement: "Set your mind on things above, not on things on the earth."[1] The apostle holds forth two things here: first the heavenly, and second the earthly. Which of them does a man prefer? "To love temporal things and to pass away with time? Or to love Christ and to live forever?"[2]

Perhaps someone will say, I will and desire both. By seeking the heavenly, I love Christ; pursuing the earthly, I cherish the world. See here how evil the pursuits of the human race are! "There is a kind of eagle that hunts in the water. Compared to the others, it is an inferior species, since it is subdued by ravens. It has one closed claw like that of a goose, with which it swims; its other claw is sharp, like that of

---

[1] Col. 3:2.

[2] Augustine, *In Evangelium Johannis tractatus* [2.10; WSA 1/14:46].

the other eagles, with which it seizes [its prey]."³ Those who want to serve both Christ and the world are like these eagles. "For they always have both the claw of an eagle and the claw of a goose, a passion for the spiritual and a passion for the earthly. They want to feed on both sides—to swim here in the pleasant currents of good fortune, but also by their spiritual powers to fly up and seize heavenly prey. But they are inferior, since they are easily subdued by the raven, an image of the devil."⁴

And those who "feared the Lord, yet had idols which they served"⁵ I see as only resembling the reprobate Samaritans. Or else they are like those "who swear oaths by the Lord, but who also swear by Milcom."⁶ They are no different from those who "falter between two opinions, wanting to serve God and Baal,"⁷ and they are not unlike men who "sow in their field with two kinds of seed."⁸ I tell you, O Christians, "forsake foolishness and live, and go in the way of understanding."⁹

59. It is impossible to serve both Christ and the world.

Man, do you have your mind set to follow Christ and the world? You are trying something impossible, since "no one can serve two masters."¹⁰ For "those who pursue temporal profit make no attempt to fight for God,"¹¹ and "anyone who does not rid himself of cupidity does not

---

³ Pliny the Elder, *Naturalis historia* 10.3. [Although Pliny does treat of various kinds of eagles, the exact quotation does not occur there. Souterius was no doubt indebted to Stapleton, *Promptuarium morale ... pars aestivalis*, 312, which seems actually to present something of a paraphrase].

⁴ Stapleton, *Promptuarium morale ... pars aestivalis*, 313.

⁵ 2 Kings 17:33.

⁶ Zeph. 1:5.

⁷ 1 Kings 18:21.

⁸ Lev. 19:19.

⁹ Prov. 9:6.

¹⁰ Matt. 6:24.

¹¹ *Corpus iuris canonici* [(Lyon, 1615), 1.47.3].

cling to the author of the good."[12] "Whoever prefers the life of the soul must contemn the life of the body, and in no way will he be able to strive after the highest unless he despises those which are lowest. But he who embraces the life of the body and casts his desires upon earth cannot gain that higher life."[13] Just as it is impossible to look at the sky with one eye while looking at the earth with the other, so you cannot love God and the world at the same time. "They do not go well together, nor tarry long in the same dwelling-place."[14] Love of God and love of the world—"the one is sacred, the other foul; the one is good, the other evil; the one is sweet, the other bitter." Therefore, "they cannot both be in one person at the same time."[15] For this reason, you should be "loyal to God alone and despise the other."[16] Hate the world; love God. "Pure and undefiled religion before God and the Father is this: to keep oneself unspotted from the world."[17] For "the filth of the world soon tastes bitter to those for whom Christ becomes sweet."[18] O Christian merchant, may your mind therefore soon be separated from the things below and set on fire by godly desires. May it be yoked to the things above, so that "it may glow with love for them, by glowing open itself, by opening itself take captive,"[19] and by taking captive urge the soul to seek the things of heaven. O how blessed is the mind that remains unmoved by earthly things, and is rather incited by what is of heaven to love God!

---

[12] *Corpus iuris canonici* [(Lyon, 1615), 1.57.7].

[13] Lactantius, *De vero cultu* [*Divinarum institutionum libri VII*] 7.5 [FC 49:487–88].

[14] Ovid, *Metamorphoses* [2; LCL 42:119].

[15] [Pseudo-]Augustine, *Meditationes* 35 [MPL 40:930].

[16] Matt. 6:24.

[17] James 1:27.

[18] [Pseudo-]Bernard of Clairvaux, *Sermo in verba sapientiae* 2 [MPL 184:1033].

[19] Gregory [could not be found].

60. There are two classes of people: the first love heaven, the second the earth. But we are to follow the former.

It has been said of old that there are two classes of men. Some were called "sons of heaven," since they "in their burning love for the spiritual enter the heavenly regions."[20] The others were called "sons of the earth." Their number is the greatest, since poetic fables (and especially Hesiod) say that "giants are the offspring of the earth."[21] For they only occupied themselves with what is of the earth, intent on food and stomach and indifferent to whatever is divine. These two classes of people are clearly depicted for us in the Word of God. The former are called "spiritual" (1 Cor. 2:15), "born again" (1 Pet. 1:23), and "sons of light" (Luke 16:8). The latter are called "carnal" (Rom. 7:14), "not born again" (John 3:3), and "sons of darkness" (Eph. 5:8). Let no one suppose any other logic in the use of these names than this, that spiritual people ought to "despise the lowliness of the earth and strain toward heaven,"[22] where "the highest good is to be sought on high."[23]

If our greatest "Pastor and Overseer of Souls"[24] impressed that pursuit upon us with the words "seek first the kingdom of God,"[25] then you need to pay attention to the kingdom of God in heaven, to which your emperor's voice is calling you. For this reason you should not fight for the world, unless you become disobedient to him and want to be stripped of what is above. For "those who only strive for what is of the earth are deprived of the divine and do not pursue them." But "those who chase what is of heaven are not stripped of them."[26] Therefore, make haste as it were one from the multitude of spiritual soldiers, to take powerful possession of the kingdom of

---

[20] Diez, *Loci communes*, [1:285 (s.v. *divitiae*)].

[21] Hesiod, [prb. *Theogonia*, 185].

[22] Lactantius, *De divino praemio* [*Divinarum institutionum libri VII*] 7.9 [FC 49:496].

[23] Ibid.

[24] [1] Peter 2:25.

[25] Matt. 6:33.

[26] John Chrysostom, *Homiliae in Genesim* 24.

heaven, "never procrastinating."[27] "Until now the kingdom of heaven suffers violence, and the violent take it by force."[28] Great also is the prudence of the Christian who after scorning and despising the love of all human things endeavors to reach the kingdom established in heaven. Therefore, "'while the spirit controls these members,' let us show an indefatigable service to God. Let us keep stations and vigils."[29] "This charge I commit to you, according to your calling, that by them you may wage the good warfare"[30]—that is, leaving behind the desires for what is of man, aspire to that better life above the heavens.

61. An argument for proving that we are to seek the heavenly taken from the very creation of man.

Let us now consider, I ask, how we are born to pursue the heavenly, rather than the earthly things of this world, as beasts do. "For man was made from earth and on earth; and yet not for the earth or for earth's sake, but for heaven and for the sake of heaven."[31]

In the first place, nature has not established anything for us to stir up love for earthly things. "It placed gold and silver beneath our feet, and bade those feet stamp down and crush everything that causes us to be stamped down and crushed."[32] Indeed, it has lifted our eyes so that we, mindful of our condition, "might withdraw from the whirlpools of a disturbing world and take anchor in the harbor of the port of salvation, and raise our eyes from earth to heaven."[33] "When our

---

[27] Erasmus, *Adagia*, [4.4.100; CWE 36:128].

[28] Matt. 11:12.

[29] Lactantius, *De divino praemio* [*Divinarum institutionum libri VII*] 7.27 [FC 49:541; the first clause is from Virgil, *Aeneid* 4.336].

[30] 1 Tim. 1:18.

[31] Lombard, *Sententiae* 2.14.6 [Silano 62].

[32] Seneca, *Epistulae morales* 94.56 [LCL 77:47].

[33] Cyprian, *Ad Donatum* [14; FC 36:19].

minds have been severed from all perishable matter,"[34] they readily ponder and desire heavenly things.

Second, nature has not made us like such earthly plants and trees, which have only a root in the earth from which they are nourished. Rather, nature "made man the opposite of trees, with a root pointing up and stretching out towards the sky, from which he draws his true nourishment."[35] Therefore, anyone who thirsts for earthly things can be said to resemble an earthly plant and to be corrupting his dignity. But if that person desires the heights of heaven, he will be a spiritual plant. What is more fitting than for a root pointing upward to be charmed and delighted by heavenly food? "Each should live according to that from which it gets its life."[36] But from what does a created man live? "Man shall not live by bread alone,"[37] but "by the food which endures to everlasting life."[38] Therefore, man ought to live in such a way in his natural surroundings that he never stops panting after spiritual and heavenly food. "[He] must despise what is frail, so that he may attain what is surely established; he must make light of earthly things, to become ennobled by heavenly things; he must flee temporal things that he may come to the things that are eternal."[39] And (as our Savior wisely admonishes us), "They should not lay up for themselves treasures on earth; but they should lay up for themselves treasures in heaven."[40] We have thus seen the kind of care to which people are stirred by their creation, and the kind of pursuit it instills on them. Those who seek their own creation's end and goal will above all be called wise.

---

[34] Seneca, *De vita beata* [actually Lactantius, *Divinarum institutionum libri VII* 1.5; FC 49:30, citing Cicero, *Tusculanae disputationes* 1.66; LCL 141:79].

[35] Plato, *Timaeus* [90A–B; LCL 234:245–46].

[36] Augustine, *Sermones ad populum* 156.6 [WSA 3/5:100].

[37] Matt. 4:4.

[38] John 6:27.

[39] Lactantius, *Epitome divinarum institutionum*, epilogue [Blakeney, 124].

[40] Matt. 6:19–20.

62. A second argument demonstrating that heavenly things are to be preferred over earthly things, drawn from the word "man," which in Greek is ἄνθρωπος.

What is more vile or contemptible, I ask, than a person who willingly neglects heaven because he explores the earth? This is demonstrated from the very meaning of the word, which I would have you consider to teach yourself. The Greeks call you ἄνθρωπος; "surely, the Greeks called you ἄνθρωπος because you look upward."[41] For ἄνθρωπος is from τό ἄνω ἀθρεῖν ("to look upward"), or, as Plato noted, he is so called as though he is an "upward looker" (ὁ ἀναθρῶν ὀπωπάς)."[42] "For when that one and only Parent of ours fashioned man, that is, an animal, intelligent and capable of reason, he raised him up from the ground and made him stand erect for the contemplation of his Maker."[43] This was expressed most aptly by the poet: "And, though all other animals are prone, and fix their gaze upon the earth, he gave to man an uplifted face and bade him stand erect and turn his face to the heavenly constellations."[44]

What do they who now descend to the base, the vile, and earthly do? "They renounce themselves and rob themselves of the name of man who do not look above but below."[45] Since there are so many of them these days, I prefer to speak loudly with a resounding voice that all people can hear these words from Persius: "How troubled is humanity! How very empty is life! O souls bent earthwards and void of celestial thoughts!"[46] They should not forget their name or reason and look with their senses to the ground, or cast their eyes downwards so as to fix them on the ground! "He gave you an erect bearing; you bend

---

[41] Lactantius, *De origine erroris* [*Divinarum institutionum libri VII*] 2.1 [FC 49:97].

[42] Plato, *Cratylus* [396B; LCL 167:49].

[43] Lactantius, *De origine erroris* [*Divinarum institutionum libri VII*] 2.1 [FC 49:96].

[44] Ovid, *Metamorphoses* 1 [LCL 42:9].

[45] Lactantius, [*Divinarum institutionum libri VII* 2.1; FC 49:97].

[46] Persius, [*Satirae* 1.1 and 2.62; LCL 91:49, 69].

yourselves down to the earth. Your lofty minds, directed with your bodies high unto their Maker, you press down to lower things, as though you were ashamed not to be born four-footed beasts." Consider how it "is not right for a heaven-directed being to be leveled with earthly ones inclining to the ground. So why do you deprive yourselves of celestial benefits and of your own will fall prone to the ground? For you are turned into miserable ones of the earth when you seek below that which you ought to have sought on high."[47] It is a most evil thing indeed "when, from the light of the highest truth and heavenly longing, we lower our eyes to inferior, darkling things."[48] Since "the shape and stature of man signify nothing else but that the mind of man ought to look there where his countenance is directed, and that his soul ought to be as upright as his body,"[49] you must abandon the things below you and lift your mind up to what is of heaven. "Despise and tread upon the earth."[50] "Look rather upon the heavens to the sight of which that Artificer, your God, has aroused you."[51] And since that is where God sits enthroned, let us not so much look with our eyes as "contemplate [him] with our minds."[52] For that is our Θεωρία ("contemplation") of all things, "which is not found in dumb animals."[53]

---

[47] Lactantius, *De origine erroris* [*Divinarum institutionum libri VII*] 2.2 [FC 49:100].

[48] Boethius, [*De consolatione philosophiae*] 5.2 [LCL 74:393].

[49] Lactantius, *De origine erroris* [*Divinarum institutionum libri VII*] 2.1 [FC 49:97].

[50] Lactantius, *De origine erroris* [*Divinarum institutionum libri VII*] 2.2 [FC 49:97].

[51] Ibid.

[52] Ibid.

[53] Lactantius, *De divino praemio* [*Divinarum institutionum libri VII*] 7.9 [FC 49:496; trans. note: I read *mutis* for *multis* as in the original text; *theoria*: *theos* is "God" in Greek].

63. A third argument preferring and commending love for heavenly things over the things below rests on the foundation of Christian regeneration.

Let each of us also consider the end of our regeneration, and reflect on why we have been ingrafted in Christ by the Spirit. For God "has saved us through the washing of regeneration and renewing of the Holy Spirit,"[54] and by saving us he "has begotten us again to a living hope."[55] "Why, then, are you subjecting yourselves to inferior things?"[56] Why "are you submitting yourselves to the earth?"[57] Why do you "reduce your worth to less than that of the lowest"?[58] "There is nothing inferior to and more lowly than the earth"[59] and nothing more glorious and surpassing than "the hope in the glory of God."[60] For this reason, we ought to spurn the earth subjected to our feet, and to aim at that hope (the goal of our regeneration), "not so much physically as morally."[61]

[1.] For he who "is now admitted to the gift of God and is (by his regeneration) next to God, whatever to others seems sublime and great in human affairs, he boasts to lie beneath his consciousness."[62] Indeed, "nothing can he now seek from the world, desire from the world, who is greater than the world."[63]

2. Next, consider in the matter of regeneration why it is that the Holy Spirit has renewed us. "So that we should walk in newness of

---

[54] Titus 3:5.

[55] 1 Peter 1:3.

[56] Lactantius, *De origine erroris* [*Divinarum institutionum libri VII*] 2.2 [FC 49:100].

[57] Ibid.

[58] Boethius, [*De consolatione philosophiae*] 2.5 [LCL 74:205].

[59] Lactantius, *De origine erroris* [*Divinarum institutionum libri VII*] 2.2 [FC 49:100].

[60] Rom. 5:2.

[61] Ambrose, *Hexaemeron libri sex* 6.2 [FC 42:233].

[62] Cyprian, *Ad Donatum* [14; FC 36:19].

[63] Ibid.

life."[64] But how is our life new? Only if "we have put off the old man with his deeds."[65] Why did he renew us through the Spirit? "So that we should serve in the newness of the Spirit."[66] What is the newness of the Spirit? It is "to put to death the deeds of the body by the Spirit, so that you will live,"[67] and "to be renewed in knowledge according to the image of him who created us."[68] Contrast this knowledge with the knowledge of and longing for earthly things. Then you will understand that the heat of carnal desires must be turned into a spiritual affect, and that nothing befits us better than gladly to lift up our downcast minds, and, like the ladder of the patriarch Jacob,[69] to touch the ground with our feet, while still reaching up to heaven with our head.

64. The fourth argument inciting us to the pursuit of heavenly things is taken, first, from the state of man in this world in need of Christ's aid; second, from the state of Christ during his sojourn on earth; and, third, from the state of Christ seated in heaven at the right hand of the Father.

[1.] For the rest, how wisely did that holy man admonish us when he said, "May you not be somewhere, but wholly there where the Master of Life is."[70] Will you say, "Where am I?" I tell you, as long as earthly things alone please you, you are on the earth, in the flesh, in the kingdom of Satan. What a dangerous place it is! Think of your enemies, for the world cries, "I will deceive"; the flesh cries, "I will corrupt"; Satan cries, "I will destroy."[71] O wretched man, where will you flee? Will you

---

[64] Rom. 6:4.
[65] Col. 3:9.
[66] Rom. 7:6.
[67] Rom. 8:13.
[68] Col. 3:10.
[69] Gen. 28:12.
[70] Augustine [could not be found].
[71] Bernard of Clairvaux, *Sermones*. [On this common attribution, see *Catechesis in the Later Middle Ages I: The* Exposition of the Lord's Prayer *of Jordan of Quedlinburg, OESA (d. 1380)*, ed. Eric Leland Saak (Leiden: Brill, 2015), 360n30.]

rush into earthly things? You will rush down. Believe me, there will be no hope of escape unless you flee back to your Redeemer, who calls out to you: "Come, I will give you rest."[72] It will confirm most clearly how displeasing earthly things are, if what is of heaven pleases you.

2. What great thing does the Master of Life want you to be in this world, so that you neglect heaven on its account? There is no such thing. This is why he "in the days of his flesh"[73] "did despise all the good things of earth, showed them as to be despised; and endured all earthly ills that he taught must be endured; so that neither might happiness be sought in the former nor unhappiness be feared in the latter."[74]

3. Consider also where the Master of Life is now. He is in heaven, at the right hand of God. "If then you were raised with Christ, seek those things which are above, where Christ is, sitting at the right hand of God."[75] He vanished from their eyes and ascended "far above all the heavens,"[76] so that believers should not look for him on earth but in heaven. For this reason, I now ask how anything human can seem sweet to a Christian man, when Christ (in whom he desires to partake) no longer can be found in them? And, moreover, how can a Christian boast that he "has been seated together in the heavenly places in Christ Jesus"[77] while on earth below he zealously pursues the things that belong to this age and are subjected to human feet? "A heart that is full of the world's affairs cannot aspire to the sweetness of such contemplation. It must die to the present age, so that it adheres to God alone by its lofty meditations and by its desires for the heavenly things."[78] Once he has perceived the rightness of these things, he will

---

[72] Matt. 11:28.

[73] Heb. 5:7.

[74] Augustine, *De catechizandis rudibus* 22 [ACW 2:70].

[75] Col. 3:1.

[76] Eph. 4:10.

[77] Eph. 2:6.

[78] Jerome, *Libellus de virginitate servanda*. [For this citation, see the spurious Jerome text known as the *Regula monachorum* 27; MPL 30:414.]

readily be overcome by disgust for and sickness of the world. For "what makes divine things so pleasant is that those who are enticed by them can easily put off their earthly desires. To be occupied with human matters is sweet—but that is for him who still has not tasted any of the joys of heaven. For the less they understand eternal things, the greater delight they take in their repose in what is temporal. But anyone who has tasted what comes from above will easily spurn earthly things."[79] It is therefore better to spurn these earthly things and to seek the things that are above. "Live, I beg, but live for God. For to live for the world is a work of death. But to live for God is a life really alive."[80]

65. The fifth argument proving that merchants ought to seek heavenly things is drawn from the words of the apostle in Philippians 3:20: "Our citizenship is in heaven ..."

In order that you, O merchant, might feel more tightly bound by a desire for the heavenly, consider your πολίτευμα, that is, as Jerome translates it, "citizenship." Where is it? The apostle teaches us this with the following words: "For our citizenship (πολίτευμα) is in heaven, from which we also eagerly wait for the Savior, the Lord Jesus Christ."[81] You have heard now that your citizenship is in heaven. But do you want "to stick to the birdlime of earthly things"?[82] You understand that your delight is located above, but do you continue to resist your happiness, too much detained by the empty felicity of the present age? The philosopher Anaxagoras could help you overcome this confusion. For whenever he "indicted over some possession or house, he used to give the plaintiff immediately what he had been seeking. And as his

---

[79] Bernard of Clairvaux, *Sermones*. [Here Souterius seems to combine three passages, two from Bernard and Climacus mentioned in Ludovicus Granatensis, *Quartus tomus concionum de tempore* (Antwerp, 1597), 309, and one from Gregory, mentioned in *Primus tomus concionum de tempore* (Antwerp, 1591), 434.]

[80] Augustine, *Epistulae* 32 [WSA 2/1:114, reading *vivera* for *vivere*].

[81] Phil. 3:20.

[82] Augustine, [*Sermones ad populum* 112.6; WSA 3/4:150].

fortune decreased with time, his friends reproached him and asked, 'Why do you not look after your fortune?'"[83] Pointing to the sky, he told them, "'That is my fatherland, that is my inheritance, that is what I look after and guard. The things that are on earth do not belong to me.'"[84] O splendid words! But if a man ignorant of the true religion uttered such things, this is all the more reason for you, a Christian, to turn your mind away from earthly matters and to attend to heaven. Or do you think it is enough just to boast of being a "fellow citizen with the saints and members of the household of God"[85] and to allow your desire for heavenly things to be snuffed out and to run after earthly things alone? If that is what you think, you are wrong, so very wrong.

Just as when someone who wants to return to his fatherland "on the way comes to an inn abounding in comforts, and, since it pleases him, wants to stay there—you would say to him, 'Man, have you forgotten your purpose?'"[86]—so I stand amazed that "this feeble lethargy has diffused such a total forgetfulness through the inmost senses."[87] "You were not traveling to this place but through it. 'But,' he will say to you again, 'This is a fine inn and well equipped.' Would you then not respond, 'And how many other inns are just as well equipped and fine? How many flowery meadows? But you must pass through all these things and travel where you had purposed to go, so as to return to your country.'"[88]

The situation in the present subject matter is quite comparable. Indeed "we are strangers and pilgrims on the earth,"[89] our fatherland is in heaven, and our dwelling place is among the angelic choirs; our life

---

[83] Diogenes Laertius, *Vitae philosophorum* 2.3.7 [LCL 184:137; taken from Juan Osorio, *Conciones*, vol. 1, *A dominica prima adventus, usque ad resurrectionem* (Antwerp, 1594), 973].

[84] Ibid.

[85] Eph. 2:19.

[86] Arrian, *Epicteti dissertationes* 2.23.36–37 [LCL 131:407].

[87] Horace, *Epodi* 14 [LCL 33:303].

[88] Arrian, *Epicteti dissertationes* [2.23.37–38; LCL 131:407].

[89] Heb. 11:13.

is a "pilgrimage to our fatherland."[90] Why then do you tarry on your journey and prefer to enjoy your place of retreat as a pilgrim, rather than to taste the sweetness of your heavenly fatherland as a citizen? On the whole, the "memory of one's fatherland is too sweet"[91] when living in a foreign land. "For the more bitter the latter tastes, the sweeter the former. From the place of one's pilgrimage grows the affection for one's own dwelling place."[92] How sweet the memory of Zion and fatherland was to the Israelites as they sat along the rivers of Babylon.[93] It drew tears from them. "By what sweet charm I know not the native land draws all men nor allows them to forget her."[94] But how much better is it in this sad and miserable pilgrimage of life to be held by the hope of the heavenly Father and a love for one's heavenly dwelling place? "Anyone who enjoys being on pilgrimage is no lover of home; if our homeland is sweet, pilgrimage is bitter."[95] If the pilgrimage is bitter, we ought not to forget our fatherland to which we do well to return with haste.[96] "Let us listen, and long to see for the city of which we are citizens, and how love of our own fatherland and city may be revived in us, which we have forgotten through being abroad so long. For our Father has sent us letters from there. God has provided the Scriptures for us, so that by these letters from him our longing to return home may be aroused."[97] For "among his fellow citizens a person ought to live more freely."[98] And we "are no longer strangers and foreigners, but fellow citizens with the saints and members of the household of God."[99]

---

[90] Gen. 47:9.

[91] Cassiodorus, *Expositio in Psalterium* 136.6.

[92] Ibid.

[93] [Cf. Ps. 137:1].

[94] Ovid, *Epistulae ex Ponto* 1.3.35–36 [LCL 151:283].

[95] Augustine, *Enarrationes in Psalmos* 85.11 [WSA 3/18:231].

[96] [Trans. note: I read *festinanter* for *festinantur*.]

[97] Augustine, *Enarrationes in Psalmos* 64.2 [WSA 3/17:267].

[98] Arrian, *Epicteti dissertationes* 2.23 [LCL 131].

[99] Eph. 2:19.

Therefore, O man, "learn in this world to be above the world, and if you have a body, may an inner wing fly in you and seek heaven."[100]

66. The sixth argument inciting to love of heavenly things is taken from the excellence of the Christian faith.

Consider next what the Christian faith places before the eyes of our mind, namely, heaven, which it exposes. Therefore, "is it not madness to seek earthly things on earth, when you have set your theater in heaven."[101] Do you not insult yourself when you allow your cupidity to stoop to these lower things? For "since they are fragile and earthly and pertain solely to the cultivation of the body, no one can be made better; no one can become more just."[102] If "you were a gentile and had no hope for anything beyond this life, it would be quite difficult perhaps to put off your love for earthly things. But now that you look out for heaven and the things that are in heaven, does that seem so difficult? If I were to say, 'Pursue riches!' you would become angry with me and say, 'How am I to do this now that I look out for heaven, from which such riches would keep me? It would be an insult to you if I put gold and precious stones before you, but tell you to strive for lead.'"[103] Watch out that you do yourself no injustice and measure your happiness not by the object of your faith, but by the enjoyment of earthly things. Indeed, I know that you consider yourself a believer, and yet "how contemptible a thing a Christian man is unless he rises above his human concerns."[104] And how weak and languid is your faith, unless you raise yourself above these earthly treasures! For it is

---

[100] Ambrose, *De virginitate* [1.18.108; MPL 16:294].

[101] Gregory [actually a somewhat free rendering of John Chrysostom, *Homiliae in epistulam ad Romanos* 17; NPNF1 11:476].

[102] Lactantius, *De false religione* [*Divinarum institutionum libri VII*] 1.1 [FC 49:15].

103 John Chrysostom, *Homiliae in Acta apostolorum* 7 [NPNF1 11:49].

[104] Seneca, *Naturales quaestiones* 2 [LCL 450:5; of course *Christianus* is added by Souterius to Seneca's text].

upon renouncing your earthly desires to pursue heavenly bliss alone and unfettered that you become most worthy of the name "believer."

Were there in the past not men of great and superior mind with whom "the name and authority of virtue had such great avail that they judged the reward of the highest good to be in virtue itself"?[105] They "despised their personal concerns"[106] in order to reach that virtue; "they deposited jewels, precious stones, and useless gold, the source of their chief affliction, into the nearest sea."[107] But how much more will Christians consider all these earthly things "loss for the sake of heaven"?[108] This is what faith commends to the senses; this is what believers always looked to and fixed their eyes upon as their great "wage and large reward."[109] For they knew that "the sum total of our happiness must not be placed in the flesh,"[110] but "that good things are those which are found in heaven, and that they are therefore substantial and eternal."[111] Let us all, "stationed in the bulwark of the whole world,"[112] after their example despise the fleeting and distracting things of this world, and, "preferring future goods to present ones, the divine to the earthly, and everlasting ones to those of short duration,"[113] by constant meditation force our way through wherever faith leads us.

---

[105] Lactantius, *De false religione* [*Divinarum institutionum libri VII*] 1.1 [FC 49:15].

[106] Ibid.

[107] Horace, *Carmina* 3.24 [LCL 33:201].

[108] Phil. 3:7.

[109] Heb. 11:26.

[110] Seneca, *Epistulae morales* 75 [actually 74.16; LCL 76:123; Souterius's text leaves out the word *felicitatis*].

[111] Ibid. [instead of Souterius's *quae in caelo collocata sunt*, Seneca writes *quae ratio dat*].

[112] Cicero, *Post reditum in senatu* [1; LCL 158:51].

[113] Lactantius, *De vero cultu* [*Divinarum institutionum libri VII*] 7.1 [FC 49:471].

67. The seventh argument teaching how highly heavenly goods are to be valued is taken from the vileness of earthly things that people desire.

[1.] How empty are human minds and blind their hearts, when people are satisfied to know and taste "only the things that meet their eyes from the outside."¹¹⁴ Indeed, they wholly neglect carefully to investigate what is beyond this world and passionately to long for them! Who would not reprove with the following words of the philosopher such emptiness: "Just a dot is this entire lower place in which all navigating takes place; a mere pinpoint is the place in which all toil, business, and warfare occurs, and where kingdoms are arranged; but infinite are the spaces of the heavens. And you have no eyes for them?"¹¹⁵ How repulsive it is when the fleeting and momentary goods and gifts of this world so seize the minds that every great thing becomes worthless before them. For consider "how you hold earthly wealth in admiration, and count them among your riches."¹¹⁶ But in vain. Did not "Democritus laugh at them as foolish, and Heraclitus weep because they were so pitiable, while Diogenes scorned them as frivolous, and Crates threw them away as burdensome"?¹¹⁷ Since they so despised the earth's gold and saw how harmful earthly things are, Christians disgracefully fall from their own Christian profession when they pursue all these things by their cupidity. "Cupidity is numbered among the vices. However, if it desires things which are earthly, it is a vice; but it is a virtue if it longs for heavenly goods."¹¹⁸ For Christians to graft this virtue onto their desires, they would do well to rid themselves of this harmful love of earthly things. "And they buy as though they did not possess, and

---

¹¹⁴ Seneca, *Epistulae morales* [could not be found].

¹¹⁵ [A rather free rendering of] Seneca, *Naturales quaestiones* [1.11; LCL 450:9].

¹¹⁶ Boethius, [*De consolatione philosophiae*] 2 [could not be found].

¹¹⁷ Erasmus, *Adagia*, [3.3.1; CWE 34:277].

¹¹⁸ Lactantius, *De vero cultu* [*Divinarum institutionum libri VII*] 6.17 [FC 49:440].

they use this world as though they did use it."[119] In this way they will have greater freedom to fly from the worthless things of the earth to what is higher and more excellent.

2. If we refuse to be taught by the examples of the pagans, let us learn from our children to turn from what is basest to the more excellent. "They play with toys and knucklebones and balls. They delight in these games and think that these things, which are imperfect for wisdom, procure them honors."[120] And, as the poet says, "The beardless youth, freed at last from his tutor, finds joy in horses and hounds and the grass of the sunny Campus, soft as wax for molding to evil."[121] "But when such a youth becomes a man, he casts them away and turns all his efforts to the management of the republic."[122] That is, "with altered aims, the age and spirit of the man seeks wealth and friends, becomes a slave to ambition, and is fearful of having done what soon it will be eager to change."[123] So too we, who up to now have admired the playthings of this world and its narrow and contemptible wealth with a childish folly, "and who, neglecting the more excellent things, have refused to use the prudence befitting (Christians) so as to place our zeal and delight in earthly things"[124]—we now (I say) ought to despise all these things "that bury our minds in the deep"[125] so that we may eagerly pursue the bliss of heaven. Why? Is it not "repulsive for a man of advanced age to sit in ashes or dust, making childish drawings"[126] and "building toy-houses, harnessing mice to a wee cart,

---

[119] 1 Cor. 7:30–31.

[120] Nilus, *Liber de monastica exercitatione* [63; MPG 79:795; these and the following quotations of Nilus are probaby taken from Diez, *Loci communes*, 2:179 (s.v. *mundi contemptus*)].

[121] Horace, *Ars poetica* [161–63; LCL 194:465].

[122] Nilus, *Liber de monastica exercitatione* [63; MPG 79:795].

[123] Horace, *Ars poetica* [166–68; LCL 194:465].

[124] Nilus, *Liber de monastica exercitatione* [63; MPG 79:795; trans. note: I read *Christianis* for *Christianus*].

[125] Ibid.

[126] Ibid.

playing odd and even, riding a long stick—if these things delighted a bearded man, lunacy would plague him."[127] The lunacy is even more repulsive and greater "if those who should be concerning themselves with the things of the other age were found rolling around in the dust of earthly things and marring the perfection of their calling by their vile pursuits."[128] You, Christian merchants, "arm yourselves with the same mind."[129] Yet may you have had enough of "fulfilling your earthly desires for your past lifetime,"[130] "serving various lusts and pleasures, living in malice and envy."[131] May you now "no longer live the rest of your time in the flesh for the lusts of men, but for the will of God,"[132] and, "reflecting upon things above and in the heavens, despise this your world as small and even tiny."[133]

68. The eighth argument is taken from the excellence of the soul. If someone gives heed to it he will readily long for heavenly rather than earthly things.

Certainly, that we should strive for that most high dwelling place by increments of divine knowledge in heavenly and sacred desire is taught us abundantly by the foremost part of a human being, namely, the soul (even if this is held by earthly flesh and the dwelling place of a prison). But what is the soul? It "draws its origin from heaven."[134] It

---

[127] Horace, *Satirae* 2.3 [LCL 194:173].

[128] Nilus, *Liber de monastica exercitatione* [63; MPG 79:795].

[129] 1 Peter 4:1.

[130] 1 Peter 4:3 [trans. note: I read *patraveritis* for *parveritis*].

[131] Titus 3:3.

[132] 1 Peter 4:2.

[133] Cicero, *Academicae quaestiones* [2.127; LCL 268:633].

[134] Lactantius, *De divino praemio* [*Divinarum institutionum libri VII*] 7.12 [FC 49:502].

is "from God who inspires unto life."[135] It is because of God, "so that it might devote itself to him alone."[136]

[1.] The first consideration therefore of the lofty origins of the human soul shows how far it falls from its dignity when it allows the bonds of earthly things to pull the mind's wing down to what is base and to tear it off. "But its ultimate servitude is when, given over to earthly things, it lapses from the possession of the reason proper to it. For when from the light of the highest truth it has lowered its eyes to inferior, darkling things, at once it is befogged by the cloud of unknowing, it is disturbed by destructive affections. By giving in and consenting to them, it strengthens that servitude which it has brought upon itself, and is in a way made captive by its freedom."[137] However, it will truly gain greater freedom if it cultivates its knowledge with heavenly things as is fitting, and if "it preserves itself in the contemplation of the divine mind."[138] For it is proper for a thing endowed with vital spirit to seek and desire nourishment that matches its nature, just as "other living creatures use senses according to the necessity of their nature. They see to it that they seek after those things which are necessary for protecting life."[139] The nourishment of the human soul, however, is not earthly but celestial. Therefore, it ought to recall its origin and nature, and seek spiritual rather than earthly things. Yet "as proof of its divinity [the soul] has this: divine things cause it pleasure."[140]

2. Moreover, since the soul is from God, why would it not live for God rather than this world? "Each should live according to that from which it gets its life. What does your flesh get its life from? Your soul. What does your soul get its life from? Your God. Let each of them live

---

[135] Lactantius, *De vero cultu* [*Divinarum institutionum libri VII*] 6.20 [FC 49:452].

[136] [Pseudo-]Augustine, *Soliloquia animae ad Deum* 20 [MPL 40:881].

[137] Boethius, [*De consolatione philosophiae*] 5.2 [LCL 74:393].

[138] Ibid.

[139] Lactantius, *De vero cultu* [*Divinarum institutionum libri VII*] 6.20 [FC 49:450].

[140] Seneca, *Naturales quaestiones* 1 [LCL 450:11].

according to its own life. The flesh has no life, but it is the soul which is the life of the flesh. The soul has no life, but it is God who is the life of the soul. So the soul ought to live according to God."[141] In order to live according to God, it must live according to his will; and to live according to his will, it must love God the Creator above all else. This is especially so since the soul was created by God in such a way that "it has nothing of earthly weight in it."[142] Why then is it pulled down to the basest things of this earth? "The soul is summoned upward by its very origin."[143] Nothing is also more worthy of its nature than if it prepares its approach to its Maker by the traces of piety itself. "When the soul gazing upon heaven recognizes its Author, higher than the sun and more sublime than all this earthly power, it begins to be that which it believes itself to be,"[144] and in a way enjoys his felicity. "So it is necessary for all the wise, those who wish to be called 'men' deservedly, to condemn frail things, to trample upon things of earth, to despise mean things, that they may be joined with God in a most blessed bond of union."[145]

3. Let us now also consider how the soul was made because of God, that is, to be delighted in the will to serve him and in the pursuit of divine worship, rather than being drawn by a love for exterior things. But, you might say, why then did God create exterior things if the mind is not allowed to use them and rejoice in these things? Let me say in a few words: "God created all exterior things for the body, the body for the soul, and the soul for himself, so that it might devote itself to him alone and love him alone, having God for comfort and those lower things for service. For whatever is contained under the vault of heaven is inferior to the human soul. It was made to possess the greatest good above, so that it might be happy in that possession;

---

[141] Augustine, *Sermones ad populum* 156.6 [WSA 3/5:100].

[142] Lactantius, *De divino praemio* [*Divinarum institutionum libri VII*] 7.12 [FC 49:501].

[143] Seneca, *Epistulae morales* 79.12 [LCL 76:207].

[144] Cyprian, *Ad Donatum* 14 [FC 36:20].

[145] Lactantius, *De ira Dei* 24 [FC 54:115].

if it adheres to that possession, surpassing its relations to all inferior things which are subject to change, it will behold with serenity the face of that eternal immortality, the vision of that supreme Majesty to which it aspires."[146] Let all therefore consider that God has given them a heavenly soul and thereby remember their duty, and let them strive to be filled and fattened not just by the basics, but also by the provisions of heaven.

69. The ninth argument encouraging the worldly merchant to seek heavenly things pertains to the Christian hope.

My wish is also that you would turn your mind to the good things offered by the Christian hope. Then (believe me) you will allow no filthy, base, or earthly thing to settle itself in you. For will anyone seduced by the hope of the best, heavenly things hold any interest for the empty things of this world? Of Alexander it is said that when he had resolved to cross over into Asia and was in the midst of his preparations, "he divided the greater part of his possessions at home and his royal revenues among his friends."[147] Perdiccas alone accepted nothing, in spite of the king's offer.[148] He asked, "What are you leaving for yourself, Alexander."[149] Alexander answered him, "High hopes." He in turn replied, "Then we also shall share in these; for it is not right to take your possessions, but right to wait in expectation of those of Darius." [150] For Alexander, the means were uncertain. But if he crossed over the strait into Asia with these hopes, how much more will the one and only true hope flourish in the Christian—the hope that "does not disappoint because the love of God has been poured out in our hearts by the Holy Spirit who was given to us"?[151] How much more, I say, will

---

[146] [Pseudo-]Augustine, *Soliloquia animae ad Deum* 20 [MPL 40:881].

[147] Plutarch, *Moralia* (On the Fortune of Alexander) [342D; LCL 305:473].

[148] [Trans. note: I read *Rege* for *Reges*.]

[149] Plutarch, *Moralia* (On the Fortune of Alexander) 342E [LCL 305:473].

[150] Ibid.

[151] Rom. 5:5.

the Christian rejoice "in hope of the glory of God"?[152] He will with even more right have to decide to expect the imperishable riches of our Lord Jesus Christ and "an inheritance incorruptible and undefiled and that does not fade away,"[153] and to receive "things that are not only deceiving because they are questionable, but are even insidious because they are sweet."[154] Therefore, "dismiss airy hopes and the struggle for wealth."[155] Pursue with that certain hope the riches of heaven, "which are delightful to live, pleasant to hold, sweet to enjoy."[156] O truly rich is he who "is filled with the treasures of the house of the Lord."[157] If you understand these things, O merchant, high-mindedly hold your hope up before your eyes so that you may disentangle yourself from earthly things and entwine yourself in heavenly desires instead.

70. The tenth argument concerns the future bliss in heaven. Since earthly things pale in comparison, merchants ought to aspire all the more to that bliss.

Finally, you, who is submerged in earthly things, lift your eyes to the bliss of heavenly glory and future happiness, so that its sweetness might lift you up above all earthly things. For we all look out for "the city to come."[158] True felicity is to have fixed the eyes of the mind on it, since we have a perfect bliss lacking in nothing there, and a happiness "of which one can never be robbed or cheated, which is not lost by shipwreck or fire, or affected by the alterations of storms or stormy periods in politics, since it is eternal."[159] "Not Babylon's

---

[152] Rom. 5:2.

[153] 1 Peter 1:4.

[154] Lactantius, *De opificio Dei* 1 [FC 54:6].

[155] Horace, *Epistulae* 1.5 [LCL 194:281].

[156] Jerome [actually from Bernard of Clairvaux's spurious *Meditationes de humana conditione* 4.11; MPL 184:492].

[157] Ps. [36:8].

[158] Heb. 13:14.

[159] Seneca's *De vita beata* [actually from Cicero, *Paradoxa Stoicorum* 6.51; LCL 349:303].

walls, which an Alexander entered, are to be compared with these, not the ramparts of Carthage or Numantia, both captured by one man's hand,"[160] not the great city of Nineveh, "besieged by Cyaxares and sacked by Astyages"[161]—"upon these earthly things the enemy has left his marks."[162] For this reason, there is no full and unblemished happiness in them. Truly good is that which is kept in heaven for the good, and prepared for those "who are good and who live their lives in piety and honesty."[163] They have in themselves a perfect happiness, "in whose comparison all the things we see here are to be reckoned as nothing."[164] How foolish it therefore is to spurn this happiness and to neglect this good, and to turn your mind to what is of this earth! "This lunacy chokes us, to thirst after the bitter taste of vices, to follow the shipwreck of this world, to bear the rule of ungodly tyranny, and no more to flock to the happiness of the saints, to the company of angels, to the celebration of heavenly exultation, and to the enjoyment of the contemplative life so that we can enter the powers of the Lord, and look upon the overflowing riches of his goodness."[165] Lest we be fools rather than lovers of heavenly things, "let us turn our minds to the things that are everlasting."[166] "We keep our gaze fixed upon these heavenly things, and scorn the earthly."[167] And for us Christians "there is no other end but to reach the kingdom that has no end."[168]

---

[160] Ibid. [actually from Seneca, *De constantia* 6.8; LCL 214:67].

[161] Franciscus Junius, [*Lectiones*] *in Ionam*, [in *Opera theologica* (Geneva, 1607), 1:968].

[162] Seneca, [*De constantia* 6.8; LCL 214:67].

[163] Plautus, *Rudens* [29; LCL 260:409].

[164] [Pseudo-]Augustine, *Soliloquia animae ad Deum* 20 [MPL 40:881].

[165] Bernard of Clairvaux, *Meditationes de humana conditione* 4.12 [MPL 184:493; trans. note: I read *Domini* for *Dominum*].

[166] Seneca, *Epistulae morales* 58.27 [LCL 75:405].

[167] Cicero, *De somnium Scipionis* [*De republica* 6.19; LCL 213:271].

[168] Augustine, *De civitate Dei* 22.30 [WSA 1/7:554].

71. On the felicity of eternal life and of the greatest bliss. It should be displayed so that its recollection makes all earthly things base.

It is a pleasure to reach out further for the splendor and sweetness of this heavenly kingdom, so that the ardent desire for and grateful recollection of these things make all earthly things base. O what a blessed kingdom that God has prepared "for those who love him"![169]

1. In this kingdom "God will be all in all."[170] What does "all" mean? "Whatever you wanted here, whatever you valued highly here, he will be that for you. Whatever you wanted here, whatever you loved to eat and drink here. He himself will be your food, he himself will be your drink; he himself will be your sun, he himself will be your moon. Did you want fragile, bodily health? He himself will be your immortality."[171]

2. In this kingdom the greatest goods are prepared. "Do you love to live? You shall have it in eternal life. Are you afraid of dying? You will not have to endure it."[172] And because it is your greatest good, "there is the greatest felicity, the greatest enjoyment, true freedom, perfect love, eternal security and a secure eternity. There is true happiness, all knowledge, every beauty, and all bliss. There is peace, piety, goodness, light, virtue, uprightness, delight, happiness, sweetness, everlasting life, glory, praise, rest, love, and sweet harmony."[173]

3. In this kingdom there are marvelous joys, whose kind and magnitude "no eye has seen, nor ear heard, nor have they entered into the heart of man."[174] Therefore, the greatness of the joys lying there, which are prepared for the pious, no sense or mind can perceive adequately. "Can any tongue teach or mind perceive the greatness of the delights awaiting us in the heavenly city—to take a place with the angelic choirs, to stand in the Creator's glory together with the most blessed

---

[169] James 1:12.

[170] 1 Cor. 15:28.

[171] Augustine, *Sermones ad populum* 158.9 [WSA 3/5:119].

[172] Augustine, *Sermones ad populum* 127.2 [WSA 3/4:282].

[173] [Pseudo-?]Bernard of Clairvaux, [*Meditationes de humana conditione* 4.12; MPL 184:493].

[174] Isa. 64:4; [1] Cor. 2:9.

spirits, to look upon the face of God, to see the unbounded light, to be untouched by fear of death, to delight in the gift of everlasting incorruptibility"?[175]

4. Once a person has seen there the full light of heavenly joy, which he now sees obscurely through the narrow paths of his mind's eyes, he will say that he had lived in darkness here: "Now we see in a mirror and dimly."[176] And yet in this mortal life a pious person regards that eternal life and that truly blessed but faraway kingdom with wonder—how great will that kingdom, that divine joy, that divine light, that heavenly possession seem to him, when he sees it in his place plainly and fully, and "face to face"?[177]

When all these things are perceived by the mind, and it quickly appears that everything that seems great in human affairs will show themselves to be NOTHING. Therefore, merchant of Christ, turn the eyes of your heart, lift your mind, and set your soul to that great bliss, so that your love of earthly things may weaken in you and finally die off. Do you consent? You are doing this rightly and so that you persevere in this design cry out loudly and spiritedly: "O you who in perpetual order govern the universe. Grant, Father, to my mind to rise to your majestic seat, grant me to wander by the source of good, grant light to see, to fix the clear sight of my mind on you. Disperse the clouding heaviness of this earthly mass and flash forth in your brightness. For, to the blessed, you are clear serenity, and quiet rest: to see you is their goal, and you, alone and same, are their beginning, victor, leader, pathway, end."[178]

---

[175] [Pseudo-]Augustine, *Sermo de symbolo* 13 [MPL 40:1197].

[176] 1 Cor. 13:12.

[177] 1 Cor. 13:12.

[178] Boethius, [*De consolatione philosophiae*] 3.9 [LCL 74:271, 275].

Conclusion

72. The conclusion of the work, admonishing merchants to reflect closely on the above duties of piety.

Thus far I have laid out some of the duties of piety and "have written as briefly as I could what I regarded as the most advantageous course of action and what I believed would be to your advantage."[1] It now remains that all who know themselves to be stained with contrary vices should hold the duties of piety up for themselves so as to imitate them and to work to correct these their evils with contrary virtues. Let anyone who examines his heart learn to see and recognize his diseases, so that he can apply the proper remedy. "And indeed this very fact is proof that my spirit is altered into something better—that it can see its own faults, of which it was previously ignorant."[2] This at the same time opens the way for the kindness and care of the divine, compassionate hand from heaven to uncover our vices so that God might cover them with his grace. Indeed "the first step to forgiveness is to recognize the sins committed."[3] For anyone who does not know that he sins, or if he knows does not admit it, does not will to be corrected. For this reason, "you must discover yourself in the wrong before you can reform yourself."[4]

---

[1] Sallust, *Epistulae ad Caesarem senem de re publica* 1 [LCL 522:527].

[2] Seneca, *Epistulae morales* 1.6 [LCL 75:25].

[3] Cyprian, *Epistulae* 59.13 [FC 51:185].

[4] Seneca, *Epistulae morales* 28.9 [LCL 75:203].

Some boast in their vices and count the evils they do among their virtues and therefore give no thought to a remedy. But if you want to be counted a Christian merchant, these things are in no way becoming of you. Instead, "as far as possible, prove yourself guilty, hunt up charges against yourself; play the part, first of accuser, then of judge, last of intercessor. At times be harsh with yourself, and pursue your improvement with great application."[5] Let these words of Pythagoras sound in your mind: "Where did I go astray? What did I accomplish? What duty did I neglect?"[6] In the same way, contemplate and examine all you do in life. "Return yourself to yourself, correct your steps, set yourself before yourself as if you were another."[7] Recall your own blemishes, which deluded you and misled others you know, and apply these our aids and remedies to yourself. Then, when you have been freed from the lure of the world and the bonds of your vices, you will win from God "the crown of faith and the prize of immortality."[8]

The End.

"Live long, farewell. If you know something better than these precepts, pass it on, my good fellow. If not, join me in following these."[9]

---

[5] Seneca, *Epistulae morales* 28.10 [LCL 75:203].

[6] Pythagoras, *Carmen aureum* [35a; LCL 527:391].

[7] [Pseudo-]Bernard of Clairvaux, *Liber de conscientia*. [*Meditationes de humana conditione* 5.14; MPL 184:494–95].

[8] Lactantius, *Epitome divinarum institutionum*, epilogue [Blakeney, 124].

[9] Horace, *Epistulae* 1.6 [LCL 194:291].

Index

accountability, 29–30
Agesilaus, 47
Agis, 49
Albius Tibullus, *Carmina*, 62
Alcibiades, 57
Alexander de Ales, *Sermones*, 55
Alexander of Alexandria, *Geniales dies*, 34, 53, 79, 82
Alexander the Great, 126, 128
Althusius, Johannes, *Politica*, x
Amantius, Bartholomaus, *Flores celebriorum sententiarum Graecarum ac Latinarum*, 83
ambition, 15–16, 60, 122
Ambrose, viii
   De officiis ministrorum, 16, 44, 45, 48, 76, 82
   De paradiso, 46
   De virginitate, 67, 119
   Expositio Evangelii secundum Lucam, 63, 86
   Hexaemeron, 113
   Sermones, 56
Anacreon of Teos, 89–99
Anaxagoras, 117
Anthony the Abbot, 63
ants, 96–97
anxiety. *See* worry.

Apuleius, *Apology*, 81, 85, 88, 94, 97
Aquilanus, Johannis, *Sermones Quadragesimales*, 61
Arabs, 34
Aratus, *Phaenomena*, 46
Aratus of Sicyon, 33
Aristides the Athenian, 48
Aristophanes, *Acharnenses*, 36
Aristotle, xvi
   Ethica nichomachea, 26
   Politica, 82, 96
Arminian controversy, xiii–xv
Arminius, Jacobus, xiv
Arnoldus, Laurentius, *Collationis philosophiae moralis cum iure scripto*, 83
Arrian, *Epicteti dissertationes*, 28, 38, 43, 77, 79, 93, 100, 101, 117, 119
Augustine, 64, 93, 114
   De agone christiano, 62
   De catechumenis, 18, 115
   De civitate Dei, 19, 20, 129
   De libero arbitrio, 81, 83
   De Trinitate, 103
   De verbis Domini, 63
   Enarrationes in Psalmos, 16, 55, 118

Index

Epistulae, 62, 65, 116
In Evangelium Johannis tractatus, 105
Sermones ad populum, 20, 27, 110, 116, 125, 129
Augustine (pseud.):
   De definitionibus, 31
   Manuale, 101
   Meditationes, 64, 107
   Sermo de symbol, 130
   Soliloquia animae ad Deum, 95, 101, 124, 126, 128
Aulus Gellius, *Noctes atticae*, 26, 51
avarice, 80, 81. See also greed.
Aventinus, Joannes, *Annalium boiarum*, 80

bankrupters, xvi
Barlaeus, Caspar, *On the Wise Merchant*, viii, xxi–xxii
Basil of Caesarea:
   Epistulae, 92
   Regulis brevioribus, 93
Basil of Caesarea (pseud.), *Constitutiones monasticae*, 16, 20
bees, x, 13, 67, 91
beneficence to poor, 71–73
   benefits, 75–76, 79–80
   Body of Christ, 74–75
   law of nature, 76–78
   to the wicked, 79–80
Bernard of Clairvaux:
   De conscientia, 18
   De consideratione, 18
   Epistulae, 62
   Liber de conscientia, 132
   Liber de gradibus humilitatis et superbiae, 62
   Sermones, 18, 45, 56, 114, 116

Bernard of Clairvaux (pseud.)
   Meditationes de humana conditione, 103, 127–29
   Sermo in verba sapientiae, 107
Bertrand, Étienne, *Consilia*, 38
Beza, Theodore, xiv
blindness, blinded, 82, 95, 99, 121
Bodin, Jean, xxi, 7
Body of Christ, 74–75
Boethius, *De consolatione philosophiae*, 16, 27, 30, 58, 90–91, 98, 100, 112–13, 121, 124, 130
Bonaventure, *Dieta salutis*, 97
brevity of life, 94–97

Caelius Rhodiginus, *Lectiones antiquae*, 45, 48, 52, 65, 67, 82
Calepino, Ambrosius, *Dictionarium*, 66
Carolus Sigonius, *Historiarum de occidentali imperio*, 56
Cassiodorus:
   Expositio in Psalterium, 118
   Variae epistolae, 78
cento technique, ix–x, xvi, 8, 13
Chalcidians, 82
children, 40–42, 122–23
Christian business ethics, xix–xx
Christian merchants, xi–xii
   earth and heaven, 106–7
   fraud, 32–33
   justice, 49–51
Christian seafarers handbooks, xx–xxi
Christ, Jesus. See Jesus Christ.
Cicero, ix, xvi, xxii
   Academicae quaestiones, 123
   De amicitia, 24

Index

De domo sua, 57, 88
De lege agraria, 65
De legibus, 28, 46
De officiis (On Duties), viii, 5, 8,
  11, 16–17, 20, 24–26, 31–33,
  35–37, 39–41, 43–44, 46–47,
  50–51, 71–72, 80, 82
De somnium Scipionis, 129
Epistulae ad Atticum, 17, 26
Epistulae ad familiares, 21
Hortensius, 12
In Verrem, 102
Paradoxa Stoicorum, 128
Post reditum in senatu, 120
Pro Archia, 96
Pro Cluentio, 17, 60, 102
Pro Flacco, 52
Pro Milone, 32
Pro Plancio, 12
Pro Rabirio Perduellionis Reo, 15
Pro Sulla, 58
Rhetorica ad Herennium, 56
Tusculanae disputationes, 17, 95,
  96, 110
Cicero (pseud.), 75, 97
Claudian, *De consulato Stilichonis*, 33
Claudius Aelianus, *Varia historia*,
  58, 67
Clement of Alexandria, *Paedagogus*,
  29
Cleonicus, 64
commerce, piety and, xi–xii
conscience, 28–29
  good, 15–18
  guilty, 20–21
contemplation, 103, 112, 115–16, 124
contentment, 85–86, 94, 96, 102–3
Coornhert, Dirck Volkertsz, xx
Cornelius, 75
Corpus iuris canonici, 106–7
Cotrugli, Benedetto, xix, xxii

Crates, 94, 121
cunning, 31–33
cupidity, 81–82, 94, 106–7, 119,
  121–22. See also greed.
Curtius, Quintus, *Historiae Alexandri*
  Magni, 16, 23, 42, 60–62,
  65–67
Cuspianus, Johannes, *De Caesaribus*
  et Imperatoribus, 90
Cyprian, *Ad Donatum*, 109, 113, 125,
  131

David, king, 63–64
deceit, 23–24, 32, 36–37
  omniscience of God and, 27–30
Democritus, 121
Demosthenes, *De corona*, 23
devil, Satan, 63, 89, 106, 114–15
Diez, Philippus, *Summa*
  praedicantium, ex
  omnibus locis communibus
  locupletissima, 64, 76, 108,
  122
Diodorus Siculus:
  Bibliotheca historica, 45
  De rebus antiquis, 36
Diogenes Laertius, 121
  Vitae philosophorum, 28, 41, 49,
  60, 80, 117
Diomedes, 39
Dubravius, Jan, *Historiae regni*
  Boiemiae, 68
Dutch East India Company, ix, xxi,
  xxiii, 57–58
Dutch Republic, viii, xii–xiii, xiv
  commercial expansion, xxii–xxiii,
  5
  Further Reformation ministers,
  xx–xxi
duty, sense of, viii–ix

135

Index

eagle, 105–6
earthly focus, 109–10, 112, 114–16, 117, 124, 129–30
   vile things, 121–24, 128
earth, sons of, 108
Egyptians, 36
   Amasis, 36
   Bocchoris, 45
   Hermes, 38
   Ptolemy, 79
   Saladin, 68
Epicurus, 103
Epiphanius, 61
Erasmus, Desiderius:
   Adagia, 23, 32, 52, 53, 109, 121
   Parabolae, sive similitudines, 97
Ethiopians, 45
Euripides, *Supplices*, 52–53
Eusebius, *Historia ecclesiastica*, 75

fame, empty, 15–16, 17–21
family reputation, 39–42, 48
Fortune, 56–57, 65–66
fraud, 24–25, 31–33, 37
Frederick III, emperor, 24
Frederick IV, emperor, 80
Fulgosus, Baptista, *De dictis factisque memorabilibus collectanea a Camillo Gilino latina facta*, 83

Gaius Vellius Paterculus, *Historiae*, 57
Galen, *De cognoscendis curandisque animi morbis*, 48
generosity, 71–72, 78–80
Germans, 34
Glaucus the Spartan, 48
God:
   beneficence to the poor, 72–73
   creation of humans, 109–10, 111–12, 125–26

   fatherly provision, 98–100
   justice, 46, 49–50, 52–53
   kingdom of, 129–30
   moral right, 35–36
   omnipresence, 29–30, 101
   omniscience, 27–30
   pride, hatred of, 59–60, 63
   providence, 97–98
good faith, 33, 35–36
Granatensis, Ludovicus, *Sylva locorum communium omnibus Verbi Domini concionaturibus*, 96
greed, 32, 81–82, 86–87
   beneficence and, 71–72
   contentment, 85–86
   resistance to, 87–88
   evil and, 82–84
Gregorius Richterus, *Axiomata politica*, 34
Gregory of Nazianzus, *Orationes*, 76
Gregory the Great, 83, 107, 116, 119
   Homiliae in Evangelia, 78
   Homiliae XL in Ezechielem, 20
   Moralia in Iob, 45, 63, 72, 84, 95, 102–3
Gyges, 25–26
Gyraldus, Lilius Gregorius:
   De re nautica libellus, 6
   Poetarum historia, 89

Haman, 60–61
happiness, 58–59, 85, 88, 119–20, 127–29
heavenly focus,
   bliss of, 127–29
   Christian faith, 119–21
   Christian hope, 126–27
   citizenship in, 116–19
   creation of humans, 109–10, 111–12, 125–26

Index

earthly focus and, 105–6, 121–23, 129–30
eternal life, 129–30
Greek ἄνθρωπος, man, 111–12
regeneration, Christian, 113–14
soul, human, 123–26
heaven, sons of, 108–9
Heraclitus, 121
Hermes the Egyptian, 38
Herod, 57
Herodotus, 7, 45, 48
Hesiod:
  Opera et dies, 27
  Theogonia, 108
Hezekiah, king, 57–58
Hippocrates, 7
Holy Spirit, 75, 98–99, 113–14, 127
Homer:
  Ilias, 33, 39
  Odyssea, 94
honesty, 34–35, 36–39, 41–42, 51
honor, 6–7, 39–40, 87
Horace:
  Ars poeticam, 122
  Carmina, 21, 36, 41, 52, 56–57, 59–60, 64, 68–69, 73, 82–88, 91, 96, 99–100, 102, 120
  Epistulae, 18, 58, 62, 86–88, 103, 127, 132
  Epodi, 35, 117
  Satirae, 40, 41, 51, 82, 90, 97, 123
Hugo of St. Victor, 55, 103
humanism, ix–xii, xiii–xiv
  apologies for commerce, xxi–xxii
human life, humans
  creation of, 109–10, 111–12, 125–26
  beneficence, 76–78, 79–80
  brevity, 94–97
  fragility, 66–67
  Greek ἄνθρωπος, man, 111–12

inconsistencies, 65–66
soul, 123–26
humility, 62–63
  cultivating, 63–64, 65–67, 68–69

Illyricus, Matthias Flacius,
  Duodecima centuria ecclesiae historicae, 80
India, 7–8, 45
integrity, 25–26
Irenaeus, "Letter to Pope Victor," 75
Isidore, *Soliloquies*, 18, 20
Isocrates, *Orationes*, 42

Jacob, 36, 87
Jerome, 93, 127
  Epistulae, 72
  Libellus de virginitate servanda, 115
Jerome (pseud.), *Epistulae*, 63, 64
Jesus Christ, 36–37
  ascension to heaven, 115–16
  heavenly focus, 108–9
  serving, and the world, 105–7
  on worry, 93–94, 99
John Chrysostom, xi, 75, 76, 100
  Homiliae in Acta apostolorum, 119
  Homiliae in epistulam ii ad Corinthios, 68
  Homiliae in epistulam ad Hebraeos, 92
  Homiliae in epistulam ad Romanos, 119
  Homiliae in epistulam ii ad Thessalonicenses, 91
  Homiliae in Genesim, 76, 108
  Homiliae in Matthaeum, 93, 98
  Policratico libro, 61
Josephus, 6, 94
Junius, Franciscus, *Lectiones in Ionam*, 128

137

Index

justice, 43–44, 83
  benefits of, 51–54
  cultivating, 46–48
  legal issues, 51–52
  love of, 44–46
  persevering in, 47–51
  pride and, 55–56
  profit and, 47–48
  reputation for, 48–49
Justinus, Marcus Junianus, *Historiarum ex Pompeio Trogo libri XLIIII*, 82
Juvenal, *Satirae*, 50, 65, 87

Kampen, xiv–xv, xvii
kindness, 75–76, 78–79
Krantz, Albert, *Sueciae*, 66

Lactantius, ix, 19n30
  De cultu vero, 73, 84
  De divino praemio, 85, 98, 108, 109, 112, 124, 125
  De falsa religione, 12, 38, 52, 119–20
  De ira Dei, 28, 29, 38, 59, 74, 125
  De iustitia, 46
  De opificio, 12, 13, 127
  De origine erroris, 46, 111–12, 113
  De vero cultu, 12, 27–28, 35, 38, 45, 72, 75–78, 80, 107, 121–22, 124
  Divinarum institutionum libri, 12, 20, 78, 110, 111
  Epitome divinarum institutionum, 35, 50, 110, 132
land, 58–59
Lang, Joseph, *Loci communes*, ix, 16, 18, 31, 47, 51, 53, 56, 61–65, 72, 75, 78, 83–84, 86, 94, 97, 102–3
Lapps, 34

lawyers, legal issues, 51–52
Leiden University, xiin11, xiii–xiv, xiii–xiv
Leo, Pope, *Sermons on the Passion of the Lord*, 83
lies, lying, 35
Lipsius, Justus, xiii, xixn27, xxi
  Politica, x, 10, 13, 18, 38, 43, 66, 68
Lombard, Peter, *Sententiae*, 109
Louis the Pious, 80
Lucanians, 34
Lucian, *Apologia*, 32
Lucretius, *De rerum natura*, 13, 67

Macrobius, *Commentarii in somnium Scipionis*, 66
Manilius, Manus, *Astronomica*, 95
Martial, 71
  Epigrammaton libri, 65
Marulus, *De institutione bene vivendi*, 75
Matthew, apostle, 87–88
Maurus, Rabanus, *Expositio in Matthaeum*, 84
mayfly, 95–96
mercantile handbooks, practical, xviii–xix
merchants, xxii, 7
  children of, 40–42
  moral duties, xviii–xix
  moral status, xi–xii
  honor of, 6–7
  humility, 62–65
  piety, 9–10, 92–93, 131–32
  pride, 55–56
  religion, 37–38
  wisdom, xxii
  worry, 90–91, 97–98
Milanese, 34
modesty, xvii, 62–63, 64, 88
moon, 65–66

Index

Nahumius, Jodocus, *Conciones in omnia Evangelia*, 47
Nebuchadnezzar, king, 61
Nilus, *Liber de monastica exercitatione*, 122, 123

Olaus Magnus, *Historia de gentibus septentrionalibus*, 34
Osorio, Juan, *Conciones*, 117
Ovid:
  Epistulae ex Ponto, 118
  Fasti, 32
  Heroides, 61, 102
  Metamorphoses, 58, 66, 107, 111

Paul, apostle, 26–27, 116–17
Persians, 34, 47
Persius, *Satirae*, 111
Peter, apostle, 87, 100–101
Philip of Macedonia, 67
philosophy and commerce, xxii
Phocion, 38–39
Phrygian, x, 8
Piccolomini, Aeneas Sylvius:
  Commentarius in orationem Alphonsi regis, 90
  In libros Antonii Panormitae ... Commentarius, 24
piety, 11–13, 131–32
  affection of, 72–73
  of merchants, 9–10, 12, 92–93, 131–32
  worry and, 92–93
pilgrimage, 117–19
Pinto, Hector, *Imagine della vita christiana overo Dialoghi morali Hector Pinto*, 92
Plato, 11, 32
  Cratylus, 111
  Laws, 25
  Republic, 25
  Timaeus, 110

Plautus:
  Captivi, 27, 34
  Cistellaria, 91
  Menaechmi, 102
  Miles gloriosus, 59
  Mostellaria, 94
  Persae, 33, 52–53
  Poenulus, 51
  Pseudolus, 11, 59, 74, 95
  Rudens, 19, 89, 128
  Stichus, 56
  Trinummus, 35
Pliny the Elder, *Naturalis historia*, 106
Pliny the Younger, *Epistulae*, 10, 15, 18, 23, 61, 71–72
Plutarch, 7, 19, 33, 48, 96
  Moralia, 19, 32, 40, 47, 49, 56, 94–95, 126
political economy, science of, xvii–xviii
Portugal, 7
possessions, 40, 56, 68–69, 97–98
  land, 58–59
power, 60
predestination, xi, xiv–xv
Praetorius, Stephan, xx
pretense, 23–24. See also deceit.
pride, 59, 59–60, 71–72
  punishment for, 60–62
  wealth and, 55–58, 65–66
profit, 26, 35, 39,
  justice and, 47–48
prosperity, 55–56, 67
Protestant, Protestantism, xiv
  ethic, xi–xii
prudence, 31–32, 37
Ptolemy, 79
Pythagoras, *Carmen aureum*, 132

139

Index

Rahewin, *Gesta Frederici imperatoris*, 80
Rampelogus, Antonius, *Figurae bibliae*, 84
reputation, 15–16
family, 39–42, 48
honor and, 39–40
justice, 48–49
Reformed Church, xiii, xiv
regeneration, Christian, 113–14
Romans, 34, 65–66, 90
Remonstrance, xiv, xvii
retail trade, xi
Reusner, Nicolas, *Symbolorum*, 16
robbers, 44, 72

Sabellicus, Marcus Antonius Coccius, *Enneades sive Rhapsodia historiarum*, 79
Saladin, 68
Sallust:
Bellum jugurthinum, 41, 42, 55, 61
De coniuratione Catilinae, 20
Demosthenes, 23
Epistulae ad Caesarem senem de re publica, 41, 83–84, 131
Oratio Cottae ad populum Romanum, 65, 67
Sallust (pseud.), *Invectiva in Ciceronem*, 25
Salvian of Marseille, *De gubernatione Dei*, 43
Satan, the devil, 63, 89, 106, 114–15
Seneca, ix, 6, 94
Ad Marciam de consolation, 68
De beneficiis, 6, 41, 78
De brevitate vitae, 94–95
De constantia, 128
De moribus, 30, 74
De otio, 11
De quatuor virtutibus cardinalibus, 33, 38, 50
De vita beata, 40, 79, 110, 128
Epistulae morales, 16–17, 28–29, 30, 48–50, 56, 68, 74, 77–79, 88, 95, 109, 120–21, 125, 128, 131–32
Hercules, 60
Naturales quaestiones, 120–21, 124
Octavia, 45
Proverbia Senecae, 38
Thyestes, 52
Seneca the Elder, *Suasoriae*, 59
Scultetus, Abraham, *Idea concionum dominicalium*, 37
Sigismund, emperor, 90
Simeon, 47
Solon, 7, 40, 96
Elegia, 27
Sombart, Werner, vii–viii
Sommerus, Johannes, *Pragmatologia*, xii
soul, human, 123–26
Souterius, Daniel, viii–ix
bankruptcy, xvi
Flushing, xii–xiii
Haarlem, xiv, xv, xvii
Kampen, xiv–xv, xvii
Reformation, xv–xvi
Remonstrance, xiv, xvii
de Souter, Jaspar, xii
wealth, xvii
speech, pretense, 23–24
spiders, 10, 13
Stapleton, Thomas, *Promptuarium morale*, 16, 20, 89, 92, 106
Stobaeus:
Florilegium, 18
Sermones, 45
Stoics, 11
Straccha, Benvenuto (Stracca), xviii–xix, 33
Tractatus de mercatura seu mercatore, 6, 7, 33, 36, 38

Index

Suetonius, *De vita Caesarum*, 78, 79
Suidas, 39, 79

Tacitus:
   Annales, 34, 43, 51, 55, 57, 60, 61, 87
   Historiae, 24, 32, 41, 42, 83, 103
Terence:
   Andria, 91
   Hauton timorumenos, 48, 49, 86, 94
   Hecyra, 33, 49, 55
Tertullian, *Apologeticum*, 30
Thales, 7, 28
Thebans, 82
theft, robbers, 35, 44, 72
Theocritus, *Idylls*, 19
Theseus, 52–53
Thomson, George, *Vindex veritatis adversus Iustum Lipsium*, 31
Thucydides, 19
   Historiae de bello Peloponnesiaco, 54
Tiberani, 45
Titus Vespasianus, emperor, 79
Totila, king of the Goths, 66
trade, benefits of, 5–7
tranquility, 102–3

Udemans, Godefridus, xxi

Valerius Maximus, *Factorum ac dictorum memorabilium*, 57
Vespasian, emperor, 78

vices, xvii, xxii, 29
   greed, 82–84, 85, 121–22
   prosperity and, 61, 67
   to virtues, 29–30, 32, 131–32
vine, 92
Virgil, 6
   Aeneid, 13, 46, 109
   Georgica, 6
virtue, virtues, 29–30, 32, 41, 120, 131–32
   cultivating, 11–13

wealth, xvii, 127
   beneficence, 71–72, 76
   death and, 68–69
   greed and, 86–87
   pride and, 55–58
   by trickery, crime, 19–21
   worry and, 89–90
wisdom, xxii, 72–73
   deceit and, 24–25, 31
worry, 95–97
   eradicating, 93–95, 100–101, 103–4
   harm of, 91–92
   providence of God, 97–98
   provision of God, 98–101
   wealth and, 89–90

Xenophon, *Anabasis*, 47

Zwinger, Theodor, *Theatrum humanae vitae*, ix, 34, 36, 39, 41, 45, 52, 63, 65, 79

Sources in Early Modern Economics, Ethics, and Law

Second Series

On the Law of Nature: A Demonstrative Method
Niels Hemmingsen

On the Duty to Keep Faith with Heretics
Martinus Becanus

The Right Use of Moral Philosophy
Pierre de la Place

Deliberation on the Cause of the Poor
Domingo de Soto

Commentary on Proverbs
Philip Melanchthon

On the Duties of Merchants
Daniel Souterius

First Series

A Treatise on the Alteration of Money
Juan de Mariana

On the Law in General
Girolamo Zanchi

On Law and Power
Johannes Althusius

On Exchange and Usury
Thomas Cajetan

On Righteousness, Oaths, and Usury: A Commentary on Psalm 15
Wolfgang Musculus

On Exchange: An Adjudicative Commentary
Martín de Azpilcueta

A Treatise on Money
Luis de Molina

The Mosaic Polity
Franciscus Junius

Of the Law of Nature
Matthew Hale

On Sale, Securities, and Insurance
Leonardus Lessius

www.ingramcontent.com/pod-product-compliance
Lightning Source LLC
Chambersburg PA
CBHW060525080526
44586CB00012B/620